GW00673837

ISBN: 9781314829082

Published by:
HardPress Publishing
8345 NW 66TH ST #2561
MIAMI FL 33166-2626

Email: info@hardpress.net
Web: http://www.hardpress.net

From an h'English Printer to an English Publisher

We beg to acknowledge receipt of your letter dated August 2nd and the copy for book.

We are returning the same to you as you have quite evidently mistaken the standing that our firm enjoys in the Printing World.

We have been established over 60 years and do not remember ever being asked to place such literature before our workspeople before, and you can rest assured that we are not going to begin now.

Thanking you for your kind enquiry,

Yours faithfully,

Printed Privately at Dijon.

A Hasty Bunch

A Hasty Bunch

UNIV. OF
CALIFORNIA

Robert Mc Almon

Backslider

Gert Northrup was rather a weird looking sort of a specimen, the other girls in town thought. While at highschool she had no chum, no fellow, and didn't seem to mind. Now and then when some awkward, queerly dressed girl came in from the country to go to highschool, Gert would stand around the hall and talk with her, for a week or so, and walk home from school with her, but she made no lasting friendships. Tall, flat, angular of hip and shoulder, with hair and eyes undecisively light brown and blue, and dresses that always hung straight about her lank limbs, there was nothing in her manner to indicate that she was dissatisfied with her make–up or her existence.

Her mother sold cakes to the town bakery and would take in stitching work when she got the chance, though she wasn't much of a needlewoman. Both of them were the sort of nondescript beings which just seems to come into existence without traceable origin of family line, or of distinct nationality. Mrs. Northrup had been known to go to church now and then, even to send a pot of beans,

673386

1

or a loaf of pressed meat, to the Methodist Ladies annual social given for charity.

There you'd see them, in Merivale, living in a cottage in a lesser settled portion of town, without any particular friends, not indulging in gossip with neighbors, simply existing. Life had been given them. They lived.

Apparently, however, a girl doesn't have to be particularly attractive to go wrong. Gert wasn't the type of girl that travelling salesmen coming to town would try to pick up; she wasn't the type even that men at the roundhouse, or town rowdies who hung about the postoffice and poolhall corner would try to start something with. You'd think to look at her that she was the sort that becomes an old maid, or perhaps marries a farmer who is a widower and has a large family to be brought up and cooked for. Even to be bad a woman generally has some joviality, quirk of noisy vulgarity or of harsh recklessness in her.

The fact remains, however that Gert, after her mother died, had the reputation of badness, and deserved it, for upon conversion at an evangelistic meeting she confessed to carnal sin. Who the men were, where they come from? — Yes, there were other girls in town, and as many men as there were girls, who had the same undistinguishing qualities as Gert, and who seemed to take life without pulsing desire, without protest, without alertness. One concludes that Gert and some of such men got

together somehow, but who furnished the impe-
tus? — accept the reality — Gert was a bad girl. It
was known that she'd almost had a baby, and had
involved a doctor in legal trouble through managing not to have one.

It was two years after her mother died, that
Dr. Johnson, the wildfire evangelist, came to Merivale, and had a huge barnlike tabernacle erected.
The tabernacle had no floor, except the ground
which was sprinkled with sawdust. It would seat
fifteen hundred people and hold twenty five hundred. Once Dr. Johnson had got under way with
his sinscathing sermons the tabernacle was crowd-
ed every night, with men and women — and
children — standing at and around the doors
trying to hear what he was saying.

All of the protestant churches in town, the
Presbyterian, the Methodist, the Unitarian, united
in an effort to bring people back to the fold,
under the roof of this Tabernacle. The ministers
and the officials of the various churches, discussed
the emotional and permanent value of conversion
by evangelism. It was conceded that while it was
a method that did not insure against backsliding, it
did bring new members into the congregations
and temporarily gave publicity to the word of
God, all of which had ultimate effects — possibly
to draw backsliders back into the fold in their old
age.

Dr Johnson was vitriolic on the subject of danc-

ing. He would leap about on the platform, purple
in the face with the exertion of his own shouting,
and with his contortionistic impressing of a point.
« Dance here on earth I tell ye, and ye hear me,
sinners, ye hear me, dance here on earth, and ye
shall dance on the coal fires of hell », he would
scream, and then would crash on his pulpit stand
with his hand, and shriek out in an ascending,
terrific voice, « the coal fires of hell, I tell ye. »

By the time he had been preaching his sermons for ten days there was no other main topic
of conversation than these evangelical services.
There were not twenty people in town who had
not been, and who didn't contemplate going
again. Even the roundhouse gang did not scoff
now, but nodded their heads and looked dubious,
since huge Jake Murray, who had always been a
whoring, brawling, bullying ruffian, had got religion and had a manner as quiet as any deacons.
Hank Simmons didn't go because he was drunk
all of the time anyway. He had been a promising
attorney once, a college man, with a brilliant
mind, and when he wasn't drunk entirely he
managed to be a bit ironical about the « Christ-
shouter at the barn ».

Gert Northrup came in one night, the night
that the evangelist was talking against dancing.
The sermon dit not phase Gert since she never
had danced, and would have had about as much
spring to her steps as a bale of hay if she had

tried. The good man however touched upon the subject of mashing, and street flirtations.

« Let me tell you, if I was a pure young girl and any street ruffian accosted me on the street with insulting remarks I would throw a handfull of red pepper in his eyes. If he wanted something warm I'd give him something hot. » The gentleman did not go so far into the matter as to advise all pure young girls to carry a bag of red pepper with them at all times to be prepared to resent such insults.

Then he was upon a subject that made Gert prick up her ears. When he hurled the following condemnation of the Unitarian religion down upon the upturned faces of his audience, she listened with open-mouthed interest. « Say not to me that Jesus was a good man, a wise man, but not the immaculately conceived son of God and of Mary. Either our Christ was the holy son of God or the bastard son of some dirty jewish whore ».

« That's putting it strong, ain't it Gertie ? » one of the roundhouse men said to Gert who was standing at the end of the tabernacle near the entry. His manner was facetious and familiar as Gert's reputation permitted it to be, however it did not cover the fact that chaos and disturbed doubts were in his soul, because he looked about him a bit frightened after having made the remark.

But it was when Dr. Johnson got to talking about the anguish of hell, the pitch, the forked

fires, the searing pointed stab of tortured con-
sciences, and then of forgiveness, and the joy —
O, the joy, the radiant envelopping happiness of
resting repentent in the glorious mercies of the
lord, cleansed, exalted uplifted, purified, and
chaste with forgiveness; ah, then it was that Gert
listened, her eyes uplifted, her face pale, a glitter
of tears on her cheeks like dew on a lily petal.
Gert was positively beautiful at the moment. One
could notice then that her profile was handsome,
her nose aquiline, her lips moulded and carved
with exquisite generousness.

So, Gert went, exalted, up the sawdust path
and sat in the front seat amongst those ready to
come to God. Near her was Mrs. Sandstrum, volup-
tuous-bodied, full-lipped, with lustrous inviting
eyes that were down-cast now as she pressed her
four year old ill-born son to her side. On Gert's
other side sat Cliff Rensch who drove an oil tank,
and spent his nights out with the Connelly girl
for no respectable reason — though Cliff wasn't
rough-mannered at all; an easy-going, kind-hearted fellow he was. Along the bench was Sal Rogers,
waitress at the railroad station, Jennie Gallagher,
cigar saleswoman at the Majestic Hotel — no one
knew where she came from, but every one knew
she needed conversion. With these notorious
people were others whose sins were less flagrant.
Mr. and Mrs. Hammer who owned a farm near
town, and who were quiet enough people but

never had been churchgoers; Chris Hansen, who owned a hardware store and was quite respectable except for swearing horribly and chewing tobacco. There were twenty people on the bench.

When the Evangelist asked these people if they wanted to confess and repent to God, they all bowed their heads in assent. One would almost think when they began to confess that, out of the fulness of their hearts and the completeness of their repentence most of them regretted that they didn't have more and worse sins to confess. Gert was less hysterical about her confession than Mrs. Sandstrum. She wrung her hands and spoke in so low a voice that Dr. Johnson could scarcely hear her, and hinted once that her repentence could not be complete if she could not speak so that he, God, and the others could hear her. Mrs. Sandstrum had screamed out hers, about carnal offenses, wringing her hands, biting her lips so that the blood came, running her hands in nervous intensity over her breast and body. Her repentence was much more satisfactory to the doctor.

After six weeks, when Dr. Johnson declared he had to go on to another city to spread the rapid-fire spirit of the Holy Ghost, he had to his credit fourteen hundred converts, out of a town of five thousand inhabitants — with adjutant farm community and some visitors from nearby onehorse towns. All of the churches banded together to tender him their grateful thanks; all of the churches opened their doors to all of the converts, the finest ladies in town stopping to converse with, patronize, and encourage Gert, Mrs. Sandstrum, Jennie Gallagher and others, on a Sunday morning when they came to church. The deacons and men members of the congregation were a little shy of encouraging the converted ladies, but extended hearty hands and offers of church offices to Cliff Rensch, Jake Murray and others. The superintendent of the First Presbyterian Church Sunday School even resigned his position to permit Jake Murray to have it, thus to insure that worthy from backsliding. There was not a protestant church in town whose congregation, of members, had not at least doubled in size.

It was found that the various collections taken during the six weeks of evangelical meetings netted eight thousand dollars, which ten times over paid all expenses of Dr. Johnson and his hymn-singer, since the churches had paid for the erection of the tabernacle.

« That's a mighty good salary isn't it ? » Rev. Sampson of the methodist church laughed nervously, and then shamefacedly, to do away with any idea that he suspected Dr. Johnson of mercenary motives added « We really ought to do something in the way of a gift to show our appreciation to Dr. Johnson », whereupon his suggestion was taken up, so that Dr. Johnson was given a typewriter on the eve of his departure, at a dinner when many speaches were made, so many that Dr. Johnson was quite unable to express himself and could only blush, and beam, and smile, and offer to shake hands.

For the first three weeks after Dr. Johnson's departure Jake Murray officiated as Sunday School Superintendant. Then he missed a Sunday. After that he missed several sundays, though he'd come around shamefacedly once in a while. His manner amongst the men at the roundhouse reverted within two weeks to one nearer his normal manner, a jovial, rather noisy one, with only an occasional bullying tone in it, now.

By the time six months had passed, however, Jake was as tough as ever, jeering and laughing at his own conversion as only a game he'd played on them damned hypocrites at the church. Gert could be seen walking up and down the street, quite as ready to take anybody on as ever. This, her conversion had done for her. It had started a friendship of a sort between her, Mrs. Sandstrum, Jennie Gallagher, and some other well known town lady characters. Now whenever she passed by Jake Murray or Cliff Rensch they'd josh her, and she'd answer back in like manner. A sort of feeling of comaraderie had sprung up between them all, so much so that nobody needed to wonder any longer who the men were that Gert sinned with.

It was even said by many that some of the staid and tried church members of the masculine persuasion, who had conversation with Gert before her backsliding, were on terms by no means distant with her. Be that as it may, more men, both of the tried and true kind, and of the trying kind, tipped or lifted their hats in a more or less surreptitious manner to Gert as she went by now.

Sing the Baby to Sleep, Marietta

Young daylight came on, more than mere light pushing aside darkness. It was a flutter of shining petals of breeze that caught and reflected brilliancy upon each others translucency, so that in the clearness of extension every object showed itself cameo-cut against the desert stretches, and the etheral sky. Only miles away, over the sky, above and cuddling the mountains, some night protested against the reign of the sun with flamingo tints, but soon the day's light was hard and shining and its sparkle was stinging to the eyes of a person in it, like rays of an infinite gem dispersing its gleam. Later, the whole atmosphere was oven–like, red, streaked with sullen white heat that swirled around and into one; heat that sweated from the ground and crushed itself down from the sky, oppressing the sensibilities of even the desert rocks. Surely the prickly cactus plants were drooping wiltedly.

In the midst of the sand stretches, huddled close together as though to protect each other from the heat and vast solitude, sat a group of thatch-

atched with worn ... in that country? Cackes, or rogerum.

12   STORIES

roofed adobe huts, around which children, swine, fowl, and dazed lazy dogs, waddled and crept, moving to find some sanctuary from the heat. Out in the corrale a short distance from the huts stood one thin horse, twitching his ears and flickering his tail in weary irritation at the flies. His appendage dangled lengthily from his belly, flapping against it occasionally on the impulse of some instinct memory.

In the doorway of one of the huts sat a great maternal woman, soft and ticklike, holding a baby to one of her breasts that extended out to him like a bubble of yeast-inflated dough. There was no peace, only desultory fretfulness, anywhere in the scene but on the face of the babe at the moment when it partook of sustenance from its mother. Other times its monkey face screwed up in red wrinkles of protest, whereupon the woman would apathetically replace its mouth to her nipple.

Another face came to the entrance of the hut; a cold-eyed, bitter-mouthed face, across which a deep scar, like a knife cut, ran from the right eye through the lips. The body of this woman was lithe and slender, and moved with a tense agility that had a hard flame quality in it, but upon her face were hardness and resentment. Two black braids hung down her back. Fine black eyebrows and a high forehead made her face appear noble, and one side of her face — where there was no slash — her lips were exquisitely carved, and glowing red. Her nostrils seem continually dilated as though she breathed in restrained anger, or other passion. At a whimper from the babe she spoke :

« Marietta you big cow, have your calf stop bleating for a while. »

« If it was yours, as you'd like to have it, you wouldn't be finding it a calf », Marietta answered her.

The colony to which these people belonged was one made up of people who had come into the desert valley as cotton pickers, or Mexicans who had come with their families to work upon the levee and on irrigation construction work. A few white men and women, drifters, lived here with the Mexicans. Half a mile away toward town, was a negro redlight district, from which only silence came, after a night of riotous noises. A little to the left of the negro section lay the town proper, where a bank, a postoffice, and a few stores made up the main portion of it.

Three years before this time the town had been made up of only a few houses, but settlers came rapidly once irrigation facilities were known of. With them had come Mathilde, the second of the two women. At the time of her arrival she had been unwell though not marred in appearance by the slash across her face. Where she came from no one bothered to ask. She was there, for her health perhaps, possibly a consumptive, and pasts do not matter in new places. In spite of her swarthy colouring she was not Mexican, but was evidently from Eastern United States to judge by her accent. One year she had taught school for a semester, but saying she detested the work she stopped at the end of a term.

Marietta's husband, José Caldera, was a six foot, deep chested, tapering waisted Mexican evidently of finer than usual Spanish extraction; it appeared from his well moulded features and body — particularly his well kept hands. Before his marriage he had tried to go with Mathilde, but she then, contemptuous of a « Mexican labourer » would have nothing to do with him. Later however she married a Joe Granger because she was tired of working for a living, and Joe had an automobile and seemed to have wealth. He was a light curly haired English–Irish–mongrel type of a white man, whom she and others soon found had run a gambling house restaurant across the border in Mexico, and was weakly influenced by any woman who came his way. Soon after marrying Mathilde he opened a restaurant in the desert town, and would whisper to men who came to eat there that « there's women up stairs ; keep it quiet though or the Mexicans will stampede the stairway. Between you and me, you know kid, you get me, » and he would chuck the men in the ribs and wink his watery blue right eye. Mathilde was aware of this, but by the time she became aware she treated Joe so contemptuously that he seldom came home to their shack in the Mexican village.

When José had married Marietta she was even then a big woman, but not without charm about her, since there was a bronze tawniness about her flesh, and resiliency to her frame, and a sparkle of humourous coquetry in her somewhere, that Joe had evidently seen in action. Within two and a half years though she had softened and spread out amazingly, and would loll about their adobe hut in phlegmatic goodnature of laziness. Nevertheless it was she who had given Mathilde the scar which she bore. That however was not due so much to Marietta's passion as Mathilde's.

One night soon after Mathilde had married Joe, there was a dance on amongst the Mexicans about the town, and Mathilde was going to it. She told her Joe that he needn't bother coming around as she'd get on better without him. In a happy mood she'd stopped José as he was coming home from work and had exchanged conversation with him.

« Hey there José, you'll take me to the dance won't you » she said foolingly. José demurred, and was shy, still retaining perhaps some of his former admiration for Mathilde, and still afraid of her for her usually contemptuous manner, not only to him but to everybody.

« Marietta wouldn't stand for it » he answered. « Trot on to your cow-woman then, Jose'; I was fooling you, stupid fellow. You needn't think I'd let you take me to the dance even if I didn't know it'd start the whole town talking », she answered.

Marietta had heard the conversation, so when José came into her house she was sullen. An easy-going, goodnatured piece generally, she wouldn't retain a grudge for any time, but she was hurt, and knowing that José had once wanted to marry Mathilde a momentary jealousy awakened in her. More however than a jealousy was a resentment at Mathilde, whom she had helped at housework and had cooked Spanish dishes for many times. Marietta felt aggrieved at nature for having made her the hulk she was, and more aggrieved at Mathilde for jeering to José about it.

If the matter had rested there, Marietta would probably have sulked for a day or so because of Mathilde and then have overlooked her jeer, such a goodnatured thing she was. In her phlegmatic mind was the knowledge that Mathilde was un-happy, and full of passions and resentments by nature, so that she wouldn't cherish a grudge at her for long but felt sorry for her rather, in her great way. But Marietta was going to the dance too, and after supper she spent almost three-quar-ters of an hour dressing, a very long time for Marietta to spend on her personal appearance now that she had a husband. She put on a dress that she hadn't worn since her marriage, and in ten months time she'd put on much flesh, not only because a baby would be coming to her in five or six months, but also because she was the nature of being who becomes flabby.

Still she managed to fret about and squirm, and pull, and twist, till she was in the gown, which buttoned up her back with much strain. Over her shoulder she threw a lace shawl, and over her head upon which her nice dark hair shone in a carefully builded coiffure she threw a mantilla. In her hair a real tortoise-shelled comb stuck — a family heirloom it was, and high, studded with jewels in a design. Having looked at herself in a glass after her toilette operations Marietta was quite complacent about herself and the sparkle of coquetry that was in her nature came to the surface, so that she was very playful with José, going up to him to pat his head, and rub his cheek with her own as he was fussing away with a linen collar. José looked at her and said : « Ain't you the grand kid tonight; you great big beautiful doll ? »

Marietta smiled, then the smile dropped from her face, and her lips trembled a bit. She didn't like his saying « you great big beautiful doll. » « That nasty tempered Mathilde isn't the only one that can look nice when she wants too », she said finally. But after a moment the sullen mood left her and her clear teeth were showing in a white and carmen flashing smile. Finally she and José were ready to start off, and José went to the corrale to harness a horse who would take them to the dancehall. So generous and forgiving was Marietta that she said : « Yes, and we'll tell Mathilde to come with us, so she won't have to walk. »

When José had gone out Marietta called across the invitation to Mathilde's shack just a few yards removed from theirs. Soon Mathilde came into the hut, and stood for a moment looking at Marietta. A mood of resentment stronger than usual had her. She'd seen José going to the corrale and had noticed how handsome he was, and how much more of a man and a gentleman he looked than her own weak-faced white man, and she remembered that she could have had him, and now that he was a labour contractor instead of a mere labourer, he was much better fixed that her Joe ever would be. She felt insulted by life, and by José for his having married Marietta and seeming now to be indifferent to her. So after looking at Marietta a time, she said :

« Look out how you breathe Marietta; you'll split the dress off you surely. »

Marietta was hurt. A struck look came into her eyes, but defiance in her nature came up within her too. She could make nasty remarks if she wanted too.

« I don't have to stand at my door asking other women's men to take me to a dance anyway — and get refused after asking », Marietta said, adding the last with a burst of triumph as she joyously remembered that José had refused.

« Ho, ho, why you great stupid hulk, don't you have the insolence to make insinuations about me », Mathilde stormed and stepped at her. Because of the suddenness of Mathilde's blazing anger, Marietta put out her hand to protect herself and hold Mathilde back, and that hand came plump against Mathilde's face because she had stepped up so rapidly. She took it as meant for a blow, and screamed in a rage, reaching out at Marietta, and tearing at her beautifully made coiffure. Marietta resisted, and Mathilde persisted, and a battle was on, with Mathilde the aggressor. In a minute or so Marietta was panting; her hair was torn down; her lovely old mantilla was torn, and she was yellow pale, very frightened, and sick feeling within her. The passionate intensity of Mathilde terrified her. Still a dogged anger smouldered in her, a sense of the injustice of the attack, and a stubborn desire to weep because of her hair, her mantilla, and all her care in dressing for the dance which had been futile now. And Mathilde still persisted in her attack as though she wanted to scratch Marietta's eyes out, or mar her skin with fingernail rips. So when Marietta's eyes fell on a pair of scissors on the table her hand clutched them, and she threatened Mathilde with them; which threatening but enraged Mathilde the more; more in lifting her hand up and shaking it back and forth with the scissors in it to frighten Mathilde back, than by intention, Marietta struck

Mathilde across the face, and gashed it deeply. Mathilde shrieked, putting her hands to her eyes, moaning and swaying. She did not faint. When José came running, startled, to see what the trouble was, Marietta was upon the floor unconscious and Mathilde was sitting on a cot, sobbing and sick, and splattered with her own blood. She told José that Marietta had attacked her with scissors. Naturally there was no dance for any of them that night.

When Marietta recovered consciousness she told José her version of the story, watching him with frightened eyes, hoping that he would believe that she hadn't mean to slash Mathilde in that way, and wouldn't think she'd jealously planned to do so. But José was silent, not knowing what to think.

Some days after in a burst of pity for Marietta who looked very ill, and wept much when alone because José came and went to and from work without many words — almost as if he disliked her — Mathilde told José that the quarrell was her fault.

« That good natured lump of flesh hasn't enough energy in her whole hulk to be jealous. She made me angry and I frightened her with my temper so she didn't know what she was doing. » Mathilde told him, and when, a week or so later, Marietta was basking in the sunlight of José's goodnature again, and learned that Mathilde was responsible, she cooked a great number of hot tamales and left them on Mathilde's doorstep, with a note beneath the pot, which read :

« These tamales aren't so hot as you are, but maybe you like them. I'm not mad at you any more. »

So within a few days Mathilde and Marietta were conversing with each other on as good terms as ever, and into Mathilde's contemptuousness had come a little respect for Marietta because she possessed a sense of humour, and wasn't small souled at all.

Within the year and a half that had passed since that time Marietta's baby had come, and Mathilde had helped her during the most trying period by cooking food for her and one time by cleaning her house for her on a Sunday. She was around Marietta's house a good deal, and when José came in would talk with him quite fami-liarly. So much so that sometimes Marietta would, in a jovial moment, suggest that they were conso-ling each other, because one had a husband who wasn't any good as a man, and the other had a wife who was too near to having a baby to be any good to a man. Marietta wasn't sure that there wasn't more grounds for her joke than her own sense of humour, but she didn't mind much, because she believed that José was a good husband and wouldn't leave her, and beyond that she didn't expect a man to be an angel. As for Mathilde, she didn't expect too much of a woman either. Marietta was an understanding soul.

By the time Marietta's baby was a few weeks old Mathilde had the habit of spending most of the daytime with Marietta, and she retained the habit simply because she tired of sitting around alone in her own shack. Marietta was used to her moods and tempers and rude remarks, and accepted them all calmly, having grown able somewhat to parry sarcasm with sarcasm.

Marietta thought she understood Mathilde, and perhaps she did. She thought Mathilde wanted her José, but not as she ever could have had José even if he weren't a married man. She wanted him a passionate, fiercely jealous lover. Marietta rested complacent in her knowledge that José was a kindhearted, jovial fellow who wouldn't bother about being a passionate lover to anybody for a long period of time. There was his work to do, the men down at the Mexican poolhall to play pool with and tell stories to. José was a good steady husband and a dependable workman, and a father of a family. He wasn't wanting any continual turmoil of romance. There weren't any men in the valley who would have remained permanently tempestuous lovers as Mathilde desired. The sullen, groping, intense unhappiness of Mathilde was of her unique nature, and Marietta concluded that it was Mathilde's fate to be intense and sullen and unhappy to the end of her days, because she herself didn't believe that life mounts to a high pitch of passion and remains there. So she accepted any unkindness from Mathilde, ironically sorry for her.

This day Marietta had noticed out of her large gentle cow eyes that Mathilde was more tormentedly torn by her sullen emotions than ever; she had seen Mathilde grip her fingernails into the palms of her hands, and catch her breath as she bit her lips in an impulse of rage at the dullness of life. It was too bad that Mathilde had the sort of temperment that wouldn't let her be sensible and not torment herself. The morning had been a beautiful one when Marietta got up to give José' his breakfast; it was hot now, but one could sit around doing nothing; the evening it would cool off a bit, and the desert night would be soft, and lovely as a flock of gorgeous plumaged birds as the sun sank behind the mountains. She was sorry for Mathilde that she couldn't be calm because things are as they are. But it was useless saying anything to her because she would storm out : « Keep quiet, keep quiet, you great placid animal; you contented barrel of lard..., don't talk to me. How your complacency smothers me ! »

About four o'clock in the afternoon, when the heat had abated somewhat, Joe, Mathilde's husband came around, and he had not been around for weeks, preferring to sleep above his restaurant. It was scant attention that he got from Mathilde who found him beneath contempt, with his foolish lieing to her, and his weak attempts at placating her with awkward affection, when she didn't care what he did with himself. « I'm going to Mexico for... » he started to tell her.

« Go to Mexico then; go to hell. I don't care. Don't disturb me telling where you're going and why. You know by now you mean nothing to me, don't you? Why do you come around? I've forgotten we're married; you forget it too », she hurled out at him in answer, and soon he went shambling off, reluctantly, as though there were something he much wanted to tell Mathilde.

Evening came on, and with it a calmer temperature, and the men returning from their work, wearied and heat worn. Out at the corrale as they unhitched their horses, and set hay and water aside for them when they had cooled off, they spoke and cursed tiredly. The dogs barked little; they too were worn out with heat. Coming into his shack José subsided into a chair and said little. After a time he slouched to a cot and rested until Marietta told him that supper was ready. Mathilde was to eat with them, and a change of mood had come upon her so that she was almost gay, and sympathetic toward José for having to work in the day's heat, and towards Marietta for being so immense and needing to stay in such a climate. After supper they sat out in the space back of the shack steps and cooled with the cooling even air. A calmness of pale violet was shedding itself upon them, as though night were a purple bud unfolding itself to reveal them the center of its chrysallis, and its hues deepened as it opened, till the night was all purple black, with not a star gleaming in the sky. Tiredness had made them all gentle and quiet. At last they retired, Mathilde going to her hut, and soon to bed, where soon she fell to sleep.

Too frequently did the dogs break into savage barking at night times for there to be much attention paid to their noises. It was about one o'clock that Mathilde was awaked by their vicious snarling and snapping, but soon she dozed off again, lightly. When at a different sound she awoke, and lay still in the dark of her hut, her sleepnumbed mind was afraid, for she knew that somebody was in the room with her. After a moment she spoke : « Who is there ; don't move or I shall shoot. »

Then her husband's voice answered « Don't pull that bluff; I know you ain't got a gun », and for the first time Mathilde was afraid of Joe. A lamp was lighted, and he said :.

« I want money, where do you keep it? You're saying you can forget our marriage, but you don't forget to take money I give you. » And Mathilde looking at him, saw that there was something unusual about him, as though he were doped, and there, in the doorway of the shack she saw another figure, that of a hardfaced negress. Joe was fumbling about in the drawer of the bureau, nervous, his hands and eyes twitching.

« I want money, I say to you », Joe answered, « her and me has got to get over the border to Mexico tonight. The cop's after us for smuggling dope. »

« There isn't any money here. Get out with that black slut, I tell you », Mathilde told him, half in great anger and half in great terror. The negress was so cruelfaced a specimen and Joe so crazed with drugs that she knew she was not dealing with normal human beings.

It was then that the negress drew a revolver, and spoke harshly « Cut the rough stuff. Us folks wants money and we's gwine to git it. »

With a quick movement Mathilde rushed at the negress to grasp the revolver and two shots were fired, so that Mathilde fell gasping upon the floor, and after a moment rested on her side. Her eyes closed : all expressions left her face. She was still. Joe and the negress looked at her but a moment then rushed to a car standing out by the roadside and drove rapidly away out into the desert. Within a short time José and Marietta arrived, and soon a posse of men collected to pursue the car, which posse José joined.

It was two hours later when José returned, and Marietta was sitting by the cot on which Mathilde lay, dead. « We got both of them but had to shoot them or let them shoot one of us », he told her. Marietta sat a moment, looking at Mathilde's face. Its eyes were closed but a tint of violet showed on

their lids and black was in dim circles about
their hollows; all the face was yellow and cold
as aged marble, but the lips, and the scar which in
lamplight seemed not a defacement.

« I will go to bed » Marietta said, as she went
toward the doorway. You stay a moment with
her; and kiss her, José, she thought she loved
you », she added, knowing too well that Mathilde
never could have been happy.

So José stood by the cotside, his heart cold with
anguish, not because he had loved Mathilde but
because her face, palely shining beneath his eyes,
was freezing for ever into his soul an image of
what he had wished she might have been. As he
entered his home he heard the baby whimpering.

« Sing the baby to sleep, Marietta. Tomorrow
will be another hot day and he will fret and be
unable to sleep all the day if he does not rest
tonight », José said.

Light Woven into Wavespray

« Everything is joy on this beach I can tell you. The girls are ready to laugh with you, and sunshine is free, very free », the Spanish boy remarked, after he'd told me that Paris was the only city that made him as happy as Mexico City. He rubbed his brown legs in the sand, running his hand up and down his thigh, perhaps because the sunshine and the salt sting of the air made him like the feel of his own body. It was evident he was proud of his body's beauty.

« In Paris they know too well when they are happy; here they are just happy. I have known lightheartedness like this but a few times — in Tampico when I was a little boy, in Mexico City when things were gay, and on this beach in other years. »

Jaredo Musice, he called himself. He had told me his name with a lingering intonation upon its syllables. I listened to him casually, because of a lack of interest I have in strangers, and also because of phrases he used such as « these people », « the crowds here », used in such a way as to give the impression that he was not one of the many, but was always an onlooker. I was tired of sophistication, and of « onlookers ». It isn't enough to look on at life and detect its unique gestures, and succeed but poorly at feeling its emotions. I hadn't come to the beach to talk to somebody with an intellect. Not while the sunshine was full of capricious caresses, and the ocean breeze came in bearing peace and vigour in its arms to lay next to my heart.

It was enough to rest on the sand desiring nothing, knowing nobody. Many children in tiny bathing suits that sagged around their skinny or plump limbs dabbled in the sand, thrust timid feet into the waves that tossed up as though playfully trying to frighten them. Some of them would cry out to their mothers occasionally, but even in the fretting and scolding of their mothers was a quality of contentment.

Then there were the young girls with modestly scant bathing suits upon them, modest enough so that there was no pretense of concealing the fact that they had nice limbs and knew it. Some of them had laughed at me; I had talked to some of them, and knew that when I felt like it, I could run out into the water and splash and be splashed by them. I didn't know but what a nice one of them would have dinner with me, and dance with me. One never knows what girls on a beach may do, until one explores.

« It was but yesterday that I have saved a woman's life — young and beautiful. She has told me I was a brave man ; that I should come and see her. » Jaredo spoke, and it flitted across my mind that I was too tired to be skeptical. « You will see her ? » I asked, since it's not hard to be gracious and one desires graciousness oneself so often. Anyway there was the sand to lie on and the sunshine to abstract oneself into.

« No, no, I shall not see her. That is done with. One should never attempt to complete such experience with intimacy. I have learned that in life. The fancy serves much better than the fact », he answered. « My God, the voice of all the tired culture in the world is speaking to me », I thought. I was weary before coming down to the beach of realizing how little satisfaction there is in facing actuality, so was not ready to take up the conversation on that strain. Consequently I said nothing.

A slow wave of apathy, akin to nausea, submerged my consciousness. It occurs to me at times that there is a pathologic quality in my aversion to people at some times, and particularly to the unknown person who makes himself an individual out of a crowd by speaking to me. Here, with the sunlight flickering in sprays of gold sandust around me I should have been of the texture of that irresponsible brightness. But one mood, sea mood, one sheen, sun sheen, and one fibre — that of the light alchemized breeze patting the brine of the ocean's rhythmic tranquillity upon the beach, fitted the place, and I had fitted the place because of *naïveté* in me, until this person — who had *naïveté* in him too for that matter — had estranged me from its quality. Like figures in a kaleidescopic design people in colored garments, in bathing suits, resting under huge beach parasols; expectant, air-sniffing. inquisitive canines, seaside candy and refreshment booths, wove themselves into the atmosphere. The occasion should have been taken for joy of light and movement, of the tint of flesh on young people exhuberant with vanity about their own symmetry; for my own momentago buoyant conceit of being... Then it struck me that I was caught at a moment of Philistinism, ready to battle with the doggedness of mediocrity not to have my little moment of contentment annihilated by the travail of thought. Indeed there is more than sheep willingness to conform in the ordinary insistence upon convention; there is terror, in a manner, that facing life more barely means the loss of much personal security, and — also of happiness. It is not amongst the conformers of life that combat is most vicious.

He had me. I was forced to converse with him, to tell him that there is such a thing as will; that one might as well complete any experience that seems desirable and take the pain of discovering its futility if there is the tedious tragedy of disillusionment in its acceptance. Fearsome inaction is a bitterer experience than any other.

The conversation was uninforming. I had known
that he was an embittered adolescent, with an
intellect that justified his unhappy emotions on the
ground of spirituality. Probably I could more than
compete with him at the little game of soul-
tormenting, but there he was, inflicted upon me
because of sympathetic understanding in me,
making me disgusted with him, with myself, while
I came back with emphasis to a disgust at life. It
was such as he that drove me away from youth
my own age to people double that age, and irritating
they were to me too because of « maturity », which
is quite generally a complacent sinking into « I
used to think that too » sort of attitude. Having, in
an attempt to bolster up his spirit, thrown myself
into the morbid agonies, I then took command
saying: « We'll forget such talk for a while. There's
too likely looking girls, let's ask them if they'll
dance with us », and suited the action to the idea.
It was necessary to go about the matter with some
subtlety — about that of an elephant's tramp
through the forest — and the girls said they would
like to dance, and were direct and un–kittenish
about their acceptance. When we had all gone into
the bathhouse and dressed, and Jaredo and I saw
them again, there was in me the self–congratula-
tory feeling that I always did have a good eye when
it came to judgments of some sorts. Very trim,
slender, and good class were both of the girls, and
the one I chose to walk with had misty grey eyes

and ashed pepper-red hair. A better humour had by now returned.

A waltz was being played at the dancehall as we entered; a heavy cadenced, deep-colored waltz, which beat into the rhythm of my emotions at once, drowning my mental will. One needs never be bothered by intellectual ideas in dancing, not when Leona — the name of the girl with me — will dance as though she, I, and the music are one, and that one a langorous rhythm. And the odour of her hair was cleanly scentless; the touch of her cheek as — as smooth as only the touch of a Leona's cheek can be. She knew how to laugh as though there is nothing but laughter. Leona is the only girl to love — Leona who one meets on a beach in California, dances and laughs with, and never sees again, because Leona is leaving for somewhere tomorrow... and it's too bad if she isn't leaving and one does see her again after having told so many friends what a beautiful girl one picked up casually.

The sun went down, but we being in the dance-hall did not see it; there was for us the music, the moment of shuffling feet and light bodies that danced delightfully, because who but good dancers would be at the beach on a weekday, and presume to get on that floor to dance to that melancholy swaying undercurrant-sobbing music of minor ecstacy?... So we danced... and later as we said good-bye to Leona, and Daisy, the sulphurous illumi-

nation that plays out over the ocean waves some
nights, only some nights, was out there this night.
Goodbye to Leona, as the mystic lights hover above
the brine and the satin swish of waves sends water
up sand on the beach to run down again, quicksilver
mirroring yellow sparkling moon and star reflections at the sky.

So Jaredo and I were left together, and when
we had walked a ways and talked some he said :
« That was a lighthearted time, wasn't it ; but then
such times accomplish nothing. »

An insistant irritation swoll within me against
Jaredo; and I knew that much of the irritation
was against him because he echoed my own
thoughts. « What is accomplishing something? »
I asked him impatiently, and my intellect was
condemning my own brooding emotions for not
taking a situation and extracting all the joyous
gaity there is in it, and accepting it for the moments
satisfaction.

From the ocean came the muted sound of a
passing ships whistle; the lap of waves softly
tossing; from the city came the dim clangor of
streetcars banging on their rails, the whisper of
voices of many people that made an irregular
insistent murmur. A few beach booth sellers still
called out their wares. Sadness lay itself upon my
spirit; I knew it had lay itself upon Jaredo's
spirit; but beneath the melancholy in us both was
driving unrest and bitterness. I could feel in his voice

that a rasp of detesting discontent with life, a harsh sense of frustration, would not let his moods be gentle inwardly. And condemnation of him arose within me, since it is so futile to storm and fret inside one self, so stupid, and little able to change conditions. To evade riding in the street-car with him back to the city I explained that I would go and stay with a friend I knew in the beachtown, and I knew no one.

Going back to town on a later car, I moped, alternately blaming myself for foolish romantic yearnings ; saying to myself that I, destesting sentimentality, was moɪe sentimental about myself — always myself — than anybody ever had been about anything else, and then I would protest to defend myself to myself that life is wrong, oppres-sive — people are dull, mercenary, and selfish — but so was I, as Jaredo had been. Together had either of our groping individual desires accepted the plight of the other to help make the passing friendliness of the moment one of sympathetic response.

I was a fool — with hungry blood, hungry spirit, and a mean narrow mind — why couldn't I understand that all people are caught, and try to give in a way I desired to get — my heart seemed running to liquid that poured through me diffusing across my chest, sinking into my stomach, a thick warm sickening liquid of sadness, that made me feel incompetent to go on — and my mind has a virulent detestation for melancholy and incompetence.

Some moments at the swelling urge of a violent protest against — against what ? — only a driving protest, it seemed that bloodvessels in me would have to burst, the cords and veins of my neck taut — would I ever be reasonable about life ?

The wind coming through the window of the streetcar was clean, and sometimes brought sweet odours to my nostrils ; the night was lovely grey flesh with an amber glow about it ; the night was peaceful — and I was riding through it, hopeless with vanities, and ambitions that I could not even locate to myself. But gradually the clear air made me feel a little happy.

Obsequies for the Dead

Now old man O'Brien, Dad O'Brien was dead.
At the fire stable they would miss his coming to sit
out on the front walk, leaning his chair against
the building while he ruminated, and smoked, and
dozed, and talked about women, and told funny
stories, and knew the life history of any person in
town who might be mentioned. Once the mayor of
the town, he'd always retained people's respect so
that many of them would still address him as
Mr. or as Mayor when his sole occuppation was
doddering around his house, and taking a stroll
down to the fire–barn to talk to the men there.
When Bennie Tolman went past Dad's house and
saw the crepe on the door the place seemed to
take on a dignity and a mystery in his mind; so
also did Dad O'Brien, now departed.

One time, at a graduating exercise of the central
highschool Bennie had sat watching the proceedings. The superintendent of the school had
spoken a short introduction; then the students of
the class came marching up the aisle, slowly, each

attempting to keep just three feet in back of the one
preceding. Some of them were consciously awkward in their new clothes; others were consciously
poised and able to act as though they were almost
bored with the occassion.All of the girls had on white
dresses, generally homemade and not too well-fitted.
After they had marched in awful solemnity to the
platform, the superintendent got up to speak again,
standing near the end of the platform so that the
light would shine on his face and so his feet were
hidden behind the vases of carnations and other
flowers piled along the edge of the platform. He
spoke to the class, and let the audience have the
benefit of his speach. These young people were
not finishing school, they were beginning — life
— and his voice said the word reverently to
impress upon their young minds the seriousness
of what it was they were beginning. Bennie who
had seen lumpish-bodied Pete Maitland walk
awkwardly up the aisle, and who now saw several
of the class looking so grotesquely intent, and
earnest, felt a desire to laugh coming over him at
the idea of these people going with exalted faces
into life, towards attainment. That idea was too
ridiculously funny to apply to Lizzie Potts, who by
name, and by structure, would always stumble and
bump and knock around everything and everybody who came into her way. But it was not until
the valedictorian of the class — a girl, always a
girl, after all girls are the best students — began to

deliver her address, and turned to face her graduating fellows, with her arms lifted as she talked
inspiredly on « living one's ideals », that Bennie
could control himself no longer. The whole occasion seemed taut, unreal, a mockery of grandeur.
He sniggered. Jimmie Wait, who sat near him took
up his snigger. That finished Bennie. He held his
nose, stuffed his handkerchief in his mouth,
thought of trying to get past people who sat
between him and the aisle to leave the hall, but in
the end he split with laughter, and his laughter
caught, so that soon all over the room sniggers,
and choking sounds were heard as young people,
and even some grown people, tried to stop laughing.

Now old man O'Brien was dead, and on Thursday morning the funeral would be held at the
tiny chapel in the cemetary, the chapel that was
rotund, and inlaid on the inside with mosaic
designs. A beautiful little chapel it was, that
seemed to purge a person who entered it of all
thoughts but, of all thoughts actually, for reverence
is not a thought but an emotion.

The Rev. Davidson was to officiate at the obsequies. The Rev. Davidson was young, not three
years out of college. His brow was a high, white
brow, still clear with his youth, as were his eyes.
His sermons were always lofty as though he had
written them as poetry is supposed to be written,
blinded with his own fervour, so that he wrote

them almost automatically, driven on by feverish ideals.

Because Dad O'Brien had been a Mason and had belonged to several other organizations, as well as because he had once been the mayor of the town, many people came to his funeral. People do not die so often and have funerals such as Ex-Mayor O'Brien was having that one can miss attending. The chapel was so full of flowers that it seemed there would hardly be room for even the chief mourners. There were cala lillies, white carnations, innumerable roses, violets, since some people remembered that Dad liked violets the best of all flowers; there were wreaths, and baskets of flowers; there was an atmosphere laden with odour of fresh blossom, and heavy with the mystic silences of death and the reverential silence which the little chapel itself imposed upon persons within it. Bennie had procured a seat; Dad O'Brien would have wanted Bennie to have a seat at his funeral because he'd whittled many a freakish boat, and man figure, for Bennie, and had said often that « You'll hear from that boy later.» Dad O'Brien had always wanted a son, and had never paid too much attention to his six daughters.

Bennie was sitting in his seat, very quietly, with his great eyes looking up towards the coffin, which was submerged in flowers, and feeling full of wonder and also of importance for having a seat in the chapel, when the chief mourners came in. They

were Mrs. O'Brien, her four married daughters and
their husbands, and her two unmarried daughters.
All of them were in black, hats, veils, dresses, and
shoes, all black, and all newly bought for the occasion. Mrs. Terwilliger, the oldest daughter, had on
a veil so long that it touched the floor, and so voluminous that it fell in folds of black mist along the
sides of her face and brought into distinct relief
the lines of her clean-cut profile. Bennie thought,
a little ashamedly too, that Mrs. Terwilliger knew
that.

Both Maggie and Rennie O'Brien though looked
funny and selfconscious; Maggie with her habit of
being noisily clownish generally; Rennie who was
so very skinny and twitchily nervous and giggly,
looked funnier than ever in the black dresses which
did not fit them at all, and queerly shaped black
hats that sat up on their heads as though placed
there on a joke. The appalling thought struck
Bennie that he might laugh, here, in this chapel,
while a funeral ceremony was being conducted.

After the chief mourners had seated themselves
in the two front rows of the little chapel, and after
silence had resumed itself so that one could hear
the breathing of people who breathed heavily, Rev.
Davidson arose. He stood, erect, grave-faced,
without a sound, for at least a minute. Then his
voice spoke, not as his voice, but almost as a prophecy speaking itself.

« Think ye not that death is the end; it is but the

regermination of the soul to be born into the everlasting. »

For another suspended moment there was complete silence in the chapel but for the careful movement of feet. « Rise up — Rise up » — the Rev. Ravidson continued, and then Bennie was horrified, because Maggie O' Brien stood up, and as the Rev. Davidson continued his speach, noting that he had not meant for her to rise up, got scarlet red in the face and sat down again. Everybody in the chapel noticed it. The other chief mourners looked pained.

In slow — profound — measured — sad–inevitable tones — the minister's voice went on :

« Think not alone of the passing of that earthly thing, flesh. There is a power that overrides all, a power that reaching down to earth, plucks from the clay of material flesh that spirit which is the flower, and the end of life. The solitary reaper has strode amongst us this day to gather in his harvest, but that harvest is not the ending, but is rather the beginning of life. As in the spring the fields are planted with barley seed, which take from the soil their sustenance, to be harvested in the fall multiplied seven times over, aye more, man is planted by death into eternity to blossom refulgently in the spirit. »

Bennie listened to the minister speaking in a slow deep voice, a chanting monotone, and the phrase « Not the end but rather the beginning

of life » stayed in his mind, reminding him of the
day at the graduation exercises when he had
laughed, helplessly. The end is always the beginning. A flood of memory was pouring into his
mind, and always of ludicrous situations. He
remembered how Dad O' Brien used to tell funny
stories, over and over again, each time with the
same droll gestures, the same mimicry that summoned up the unique personality and situation to
one's mind so that one had to laugh at the story
no matter how many times one had heard it before.
He remembered how Dad used to talk about town
politics, and more than that, how he'd stop Rev.
Davidson and get into a profound discussion upon
theological problems, winking to Bennie out of his
left eye, and grimacing with the left side of his
mouth too with a knowing look. Bennie found it
impossible to conceive of Dad' s spirit as a flower
plucked. A sense of the absurdity, the grandiloquence of these obsequies ; a memory of Dad's
chuckling at the Mason's for their love of pomp
and ceremony ; came into Bennie ; and all the time
an awe of death, a knowledge of the reverential
mental tension of all the people in the chapel, was
in him. He felt a desire to hide his face, not to
weep, too strange a feeling of wonderment was in
him to weep, but to try and shut out everything
from in front of his eyes, and to hear no sound, not
even of the minister's voice, so that he could try
and realize what death is.

Then his eyes wandered to Maggie O' Brien. She was sitting with her eyes wide open, gaping up at the Rev. Davidson. Her mouth was open, and her lower lip drooped so that her face looked foolish; and Bennie recalled that Maggie was forever taking off people for looking ridiculous. A snicker came up in him, just a catch of breath, a catch of an emotion between an impulse to weep weakly for not being able to comprehend death, and that Dad was actually dead, and a hysterical desire to laugh. Someone near him looked at him frowningly, and the solemnity of her countenanee struck Bennie as weirdly funny, so that another snicker rose up in him, and was preceded by several painful catches of breath in his effort to restrain himself.

Now he recalled with a rush how drolly Dad O' Brien had talked about old Jake Miller's funeral, and the sermon the minister had preached at it. « Why the old soak' s preserved in whiskey for eternity; that's it, when a man dies give him wings; I can' t see old Jake fluttering very lightly upwards with that bay window of hisn, but give him wings. »

Now here was old Dad O' Brien, who had never had respect for anything, who would joke about all things sacred, and jolly along every parson in town, who made not a pretence of having honour for the dead, here he was and rites were being held over his remains, with reverential grandiloquence. The whole affair seemed to Bennie unreal, stiffly

pompous — the performance of wooden puppets —
and his giggles were overcoming him, so that he
couldn't restrain himself from breaking out into
a long laugh. He held his breath, gasped, put his
hand into his mouth, and getting down from his
seat, tried to squirm past people in his way to the
aisle. Mrs. Harper looked fiercely at him as though
she were enraged ; Mrs. Macalester caught his eyes,
and Bennie saw that she too understood why he
wanted to laugh and that made it more difficult
than ever for him to control himself until he was
outside. Finally he reached the aisle, and went
down it to the door of the chapel. Just as he reached
the door an explosive sound broke from him, and
then he bolted out, but everybody had heard the
giggle, and many of those who heard remembered
Bennie's having laughed at the graduating exercise, and knew why. A feeling of hysterical laughter
was in the air. From several places in the chapel a
repressed choke of laughter came. Kate Love rose
and went to the door; soon Bill Cook came after.
Others came too. Outside Bennie was sitting on
the walk doubled up with laughing, and every new
person that came out set him off again, so that he
could not stop himself. Kate Love was laughing too,
and almost in tears of mortification because she
was laughing at such an occasion and couldn't
stop herself. Bill Cook was laughing and sometimes
when he could stop for a moment he'd curse, and
say to Bennie « You damned rattlebrained kid,

I feel like walloping you. Stop giggling, for God's sake, stop giggling » and that would send Bennie off into another gale of uncontrollable laughter, whereupon Bill and Kate would start anew.

By the time the services were over Bennie had gone home. The next day Mrs. Harper came to call on his mother, and was very haughty to Bennie, who opened the door for her. She spoke severely to Bennie's mother, saying that the whole affair was a disgrace. So Bennie's mother called him, and scolded him for a moment, till Mrs. Harper took the matter out of her hands, and began to talk to Bennie. He listened for a time, then recalling that Mrs. Harper had no particular reason for being at the funeral since she was not a friend of any of the O'Brien's, he spoke, highly indignant at her because he had no ground whatever upon which to defend his silliness.

« As long as people like you will attend funerals and weddings for something to talk about you hadn't ought to object to my being disgraceful enough to laugh at them, because that furnishes you enough shock to keep you scandalized for several weeks of gossip », and then Bennie left the room. And lucky it was for Bennie that his father was out of town or he'd have gotten the threshing of his life.

Elsie

For a girl only fourteen years old Elsie was tremendous, with more height than an average full grown woman has, and shoulders narrower than her hips. « An over-developed body and an under-developed mind », Mrs. Wilson said of her, by the time she had had her from the State Orphans Home for a year. But it's easy to accuse people of not having a « mind », as that is a thing that can't be taped or weighed.

Because of her two boys, four and seven years old, Mrs. Wilson was glad that Elsie didn't want to go school, and besides keeping an eye on the youngsters, bathing them, putting them to bed, and stopping them from quarrelling overmuch with each other, Elsie could wash dishes, sweep, and give Doctor Wilson his coffee and toast in the morning in not too bad a shape. Of course she couldn't be depended upon to do much other cooking; an irresponsible, exclamatorily shy and awkward being she was. The doctor though wasn't finicky about his food; he was too tired physically,

too tolerant of all kinds of human weaknesses, and
too tormentedly dubious about the various values
in life, to be anything but whimsical in his attitude towards Elsie. « She's beginning to feel her
oats now. Let her giggle and moon about. Maybe
some farmer will marry her in a year or so. With
a body her size she needs a farm to move about
in », he'd say.

As a local newspaper write-up had once said of
Dr. Wilson, he'd « taken to writing poetry »; and
doctors aren't the only one who catch that disease.
Through his naive interest in humanity and in
their emotions, the doctor was apt to treat Elsie
with facetious friendliness, that however, had no
feeling of superiority within it. Sometimes he
would joke her about a grocery delivery boy at
whom he declared she looked with amorous eyes;
another time he might pat her on the shoulder.
Once he put his forefinger on her stomach simply
to see whether that would embarrass her. This
treatment permitted Elsie to be more tempermental with him than she was with Mrs. Wilson, so
that if he was ever cross with her, because of tired
irritation, she would remark « aren't you awful,
talking to me that way? » The fact that Elsie was
always gasping because some question to her, or
attention turned upon her, made her self-conscious
so that she blushed, and blushed, did not prevent
her speaking her mind.

It was when Donald Matthews came out to see

Doctor and spend an evening discussing life, poetry, stupidity, and other kindred themes, that Elsie really began to blush, and hang bashfully just outside of the door of the dining room or of the sitting room, where the others happened to be sitting. « Elsie says she thinks it sounds horrible to hear you swear; she doesn't mind my swearing at all », the Doctor told Donald one day, and they all laughed at her maidenly romanticism.

One day when Don called up the house Elsie answered the 'phone, and said that she was the only one at home. After Don had left word for the doctor to call him up Elsie made some remark that he couldn't catch until she had repeated it three times. She seemed excited, as if she were being daring. At last he understood. « I made my first batch of bread today, and it turned out wonderful. Isn't that grand », she had said.

« Well, well, Elsie, good for you; keep that up, and when you become a fine cook you can get a job in some big restaurant, and take me on as a husband to support. Lord knows I don't like taking care of myself. »

« O, o, Mr. Matthews, aren't you a tease », Elsie stuttered so that Don could visualize her blushing twenty miles away.

Whenever Donald called up the house, and particularly whenever he came out to spend the night with the Wilsons, Elsie would announce his approach palpitatingly, and would these times be anxious to know what there was to have for dinner. Whenever she did any thing awkward and got scolded by Mrs. Wilson she would beg her not to tell Mr. Matthews anyway. One night when both Donald and Dr. Wilson urged her to come in and tell them about her various experiences as an orphan, and Mrs. Wilson too was humourously goodnatured with her in spite of the fact that she was always breaking dishes and forgetting to do everything she'd been told to, Elsie finally came, protestantly shy, and exclaiming that she just couldn't, she was too embarrassed. However they got her to talking.

She told them about a Pennsylvania Dutch family she'd been in just the year before coming to them, in which only the women worked, while the oldest boy — twenty eight years old — came storming home drunk three or four times a week, and cursed horribly at everybody — but Elsie, whom he'd look at almost as if she wasn't such a nonentity to him as womenfolk in general were. Elsie said she wouldn't stand for any of his cursing at her; she'd have walked right out of the house. The home before that they'd worked the life out of her, the crotchety old man and woman that they were. Elsie intended to stay where she was, because she knew a good thing when she saw it.

Mrs. Wilson was feeling unwell though, and added to Elsie's awkward incompetence, was a habit she had of eating candy that the Doctor would bring for Mrs. Wilson, if it were left about. Stockings, and pieces of lace would be missing now and then. So Mrs. Wilson would have to lay down the law to Elsie frequently, and as time went on she brooded quite a little. One night, when Donald had come to spend the weekend with the Wilsons, a note was on the backdoor which the doctor found as he came in from a case, worn out with having helped another infant into the world.

« Please don't lock the back door. I will when I come in. I have gone out for a walk. I want to think », the note read.

« She'd better think, the careless child », Mrs. Wilson said. « I told her I was thinking of letting her go back to the Orphans Home. »

Elsie, knowing she basked in the disfavour of Mrs. Wilson, and perhaps of the Doctor too, since he didn't like having her eat candy which he'd purchased to buy his wife's goodwill with, awed a bit as he was by the lady's manners, more positive and decisive than his own, tried to be careful and was tormentedly anxious to please.

Returning home one night from a moving picture show the Wilsons called to Elsie who was not in the front room. There was no answer. They called again. No answer.

« You remember she said before we went out that she just knew burglars were going to be here tonight — felt it in her blood. She's probably

locked in her room, scared because of notices she's
been seeing in the paper», Doctor Wilson commented and went to her room to knock at the door.
While there Mrs.Wilson, who'd gone to the kitchen,
called excitedly, so he ran downstairs to her.
There was Elsie, on the floor, tied hands and feet,
with her mouth gagged, and a rope about her bind-
ing her to the pipe beneath the kitchen sink. They
loosed her, and she told them that three men had
come in, but she didn't believe that they'd taken
anything because she felt that they were coming
and had put the family silver in the furnace down-
tairs, there being no fire in it.

« Isn't it lucky that I felt it in my bones
though », Elsie said, and her eyes were big. She
was delighted when they praised her courage and
presence of mind. When a policeman arrived that
Mrs. Wilson had asked for by telephone, he asked
Elsie many questions. An unusual policeman was
he. At last he took Dr. Wilson aside, and said :
« She did it herself; she wanted you to praise
her. We get cases like this every now and then.
One came up a couple of weeks ago out in the
suburbs with a fellow who wanted his girl to
think he was a hero and blacked his own eye so
his story of attack would sound more likely. »

When Dr. and Mrs. Wilson talked it over every
sign indicated that the policeman was right, so
the next morning Dr. Wilson faced Elsie with an
accusation, and twitted her. In the end she admitt-

ed that she had done it all herself. So when Mrs. Wilson was sure, from Elsie's admission, she declared that the girl wasn't right in her mind.

« But please don't, O Mrs. Wilson, please don't tell Mr. Matthews about it », Elsie begged. Mrs. Wilson was noncommital.

When Doctor Wilson went out into the kitchen a little later on his way out to the garage for the auto to drive to a patient, Elsie giggled.

« You'll have to admit that I acted my part well though, now won't you? »

It was in the afternoon of the same day that Donald Matthews arrived, and Elsie was as upset with palpitating emotions as ever when she opened the door to him. An hour later when Dr. Wilson told her that he'd shown Donald some poems which she had written — she had been reading the Doctor's books, Dowson particularly, and some others she picked up, love poems — and Donald had said : « They're nearer to the way it's done than some esthetic youths who faint with delicate emotion over coloured shadows will ever get », Elsie seemed scarcely able to contain herself.

At the dinner table Donald broke news to the family. « Well — I suppose I might as well spill the dope now. I was married this afternoon and depart for a honeymoon right away. Sudden, but that's the way to do things. »

Dr. and Mrs. Wilson weren't over-amazed. One

gets to accepting things without undue exclamation after a certain amount of experience, but
Elsie dropped the platter of meat she was carrying
so that it plumped on the table. Fortunately no
gravey spilled. Donald, and the Wilsons exchanged
amused glances, and a little later when Mrs. Wilson came back from a trip she'd made to the
kitchen for salad she whispered « Elsie says she
never could stand a man who wore a green tie
anyway. It's that green tie you have on today
that's ruined you with Elsie. »

From that time on Elsie was quite sullen with
Mrs. Wilson, and said she'd just as soon go back
to the Orphans Home, since she was tired of
working like a truckhorse. She also declared that
she was through with poets and poetry forever.
They never do have any sense anyway.

A Boy's Discovery

Harry Wright was a delicate boy; even more delicate than the rest of his family. In spite of the fact that his sister Nellie was pale — O pale, pale — there was the promise of a glow beneath the eggshell smoothness of her cheeks, and her wistful eyes could sparkle, so that her pallor and delicacy simply made her beauty more precious. Possibly if Harry had lived past ten years old he would have become stronger, but at nine, just six months before he caught lockjaw and died in agony, he was a frail, slender-limbed lad, with gray eyes that seemed never able to open wider in wonderment at things in life, so great was the wonder in them at all times. There was quality too withdrawn about him however for him to be lovable in the way of ordinary affection.

Mr. Wright had come to South Dakota years before because he had only one lung left, and doctors said he'd be fortunate if he lived six months more though it's had to understand why doctors will insist upon it being so much more

fortunate to live, than to die. The country air, and
the climate, apparently cured him, for after twenty
years he was alive, and with no noticeable trace
of tuberculosis in him. A year after he had arrived
he had married, and much worry about himself and
about managing his affairs in general were taken
of his hands, for Mrs. Wright was a grand and
capable woman, out of Chicago. She rented out
farms he had come to own, managed their little
department store in the small village of Lansing.
Every Sunday she would go to church, always in
a much finer black dress than other mothers wore,
and they all wore black silk or satin dresses to
church, believing it not seemly for mothers of
families to appear in giddy colours. Mrs. Wright's
dresses though were criticized somewhat, but
quietly, because she was haughty and indifferent
to people, anyone could judge, though her manner
was cou teous even if it was aloof. But her dresses
were usually of fine black lace, and she wore a
bustle that made the folds of material in her gown
stand out around her hips, long after bustles had
passed out of style. Her hats too were modish, not
in the style of the day, but in a distinctive way, and
upon her hands she wore fine lace gloves. The train
of her dress was generally long enough to sweep
the church floor and soil itself on the dust there.

Mr. Wright, following her absentedmindedly,
with his weak eyes trying to strain ahead through
very thick glasses, was like a trusting, utterly

helpless, dog, blind with old age. If Harry had been left to Mr. Wright's care alone, the boy would have poisoned himself at once eating candy from the stock kept in their stores, and gorging on fruit all of the time, so that he never would eat at meal-times, which Mrs. Wright found it hard to compel him to do anyway. Harry had always been a frail child, and not disobedient, but not happy. Everything that could be done for him was done. He read much, didn't care for toys, and didn't know how to play with other children in town, who were always a little rowdy, and mischievous as though they believed that it is necessary to be that so people will remark « boys will be boys ». Harry didn't like wetting his clothes, or muddying his shoes, because these things felt uncomfortable and he knew they might make him sick. He didn't like to tie cans to the tails of dogs, because that didn't make him split with laughter; it only made him sorry for the dogs.

All in all Mrs. Wright was delighted when Harold Morris came to town, and Harry seemed able to get on capitally with him, for Harold, while delicate looking too, was able to take care of himself with other boys in town, and wouldn't stand for being called « sissy ». After a while he wouldn't stand for having Harry called that either, because he realized how much sickness Harry had had all his life. Strangers seeing the two of them together mistook them for brothers, perhaps twins, for Harry was usually flushed and excited and nervously happy when he was with Harold, since he was at these times always learning things he hadn't known before, and playing games such as doctor, or lawyer, or minister, or some game that Harold would invent so they wouldn't have to run about too much since Harry always tired when he tried to climb to the top of the town elevator to get young pigeons, and one time had nearly fainted halfway up the town watering pipe which stood over a hundred feet high in the air. By the time Harold had held him up, and helped him down from that he never again would lead him into anything that took much daring or strength.

Summer was on, and vacation. Through the days all the boys in town would play about main street, catching rides on farm wagons and buggies coming and going from town, or performing stunts on the iron bars that ran between hitching posts in front of the village grocery stores. There weren't more than ten boys of their age in town since the whole population of Lansing was but two hundred people. Sometimes they'd roll their pants up as far as possible and wade in the pond down by the mill, or straddle a log and row; again they'd go out into the country and of course by the time they'd gotten out a ways some of them would tire, or would be afraid they'd get a licking from their mothers and would turn back. So often Harold and Harry were left to go on alone, which Harry could never have

done by himself, but Mrs. Wright had decided that
Harold could take care of both of them. Naturally
Harry looked to Harold for information, and asked
him questions he'd always been shy of asking older
people, and wouldn't because of boyish contempt,
ask other boys — Tuffy Thomas, Gordon Rensch,
Wallace Spear.

About a quarter of a mile out of town was a farm
where they could stop and get milk to drink —
sweet milk or buttermilk : The daughter of the
family was a « Mrs. » Richardson, who had a boy
three years old, and who worked for Harold's
mother sometimes, sewing, or washing. Harold
rather understood why his mother said of her that
« she shouldn't have to pay forever for an error made
when she was so young a girl as sixteen », but he
had little curiosity. He liked Mrs. Richardson, and
she would always give him cake, and buttermilk,
whenever he came out to the farm to see her. Her
father and mother were kind to him too, rather
liking to have him call on them, because that indicated that his folks did not dissaprove of their
daughter over-much, they thought.

As summer deepened, and there had been no
rain for weeks, almost every day would find Harold
and Harry at this farm, because the village streets
were a foot deep in dust so that it was no fun catch
ing rides, or playing on the bars between hitching-
posts. Mrs. Wright, and Harold's folks came to
know that if the boys weren't home at noon, and

weren't home till seven o' clock at night, they were safe, and would get their meals at the farm.

The grain fields were ripening about the farm. The boys would sit and dream stories of their future to each other. A pulsation and vibration of clear life and light was about in the clover-scented air ; even about the barns was a clean odour, a mixture of fresh hays and of fresh manure.

« I like the odour of horse manure, and it isn't dirty, it's only made up of grainseed husks, and hay. You just think it's dirty because of how it comes about », Harold would say sometimes.

For an hour at a time they would rest in the shade of a haystack without speaking, still widely awake, and alertly conscious of each other, of nature, of life. The silence seemed potential with great significence. Out in the pasture they could see cattle browsing, or resting as they chewed their cuds complacently — arrogantly disdainful some of them. — On the other side of a fence dusty sheep were pastured, and bleated, as they strolled about nipping on dry, hooftrod grass that they'd nipped close to the earth ; in an individual pasture was a bronze-coloured bull, that at times would paw the earth sullenly, lowing ominously. Off the side of his pasture was another in which a bay stallion was kept, and at times it would stand with his head lifted high up, its eyes dilated, as it snorted and neighed, and its mane was blowing as it stood in the wind. In the farm yard were many trees, all

green with foliage. The umbrella trees seemed a
green eruption like a spring that spurted a thick
green spray which fell in equal arches on all sides.
Across the road, as a background to the farm
house, was a forest which ran for a quarter of a
mile, and was for that space a green avalanche
which flooded the landscape. If the boys went into
that woods they saw many birds, and would follow
some of the flamingly beautiful ones. A golden
oriole would flit, flame-bosomed, through the dark
green foliage; a goldfinch would cheep and flutter
about ; rose gross-beaks, scarlet tanagers, olive
kinglets, brown thrushes, came fleetingly, and some
of them would hop and flutter about on the spongy
mosslike soil in the woods for a time. Pungent
odour and life all fresh was about everywhere.

The wheat fields were ripening, caressed to sleek
maturity by the sun as a calf is licked by the
tongue of its fond mother, and upon its bosom the
sunlight poured and rippled so that across its gold
expanse was continual gentle breathing. Young
turkeys went hopping and fluttering over fences
into pastures, searching for bugs, and worms.

« You and I will have to be together always
won't we Harold ? » Harry would comment sometimes, and looking at Harry's face in answer a
feeling of sorrow would be in Harold, because he
didn't know that he even liked Harry, or was anything but sorry for him. He felt that Harry was
somebody that needed to be taken care of, and that

next time the family moved — Harold's family
was always moving — he'd remember him as he
remembered Lloyd of a year ago, dimly, as though
he were hardly a real person.

« I have never loved anybody like I do you. I
don't like people », Harry would say again.

« How do you know ? How could you love people
— your mother and father who always give you
medecine, and those kids in town who tear
around — you never are with them to know them
like you have been with me », Harold would answer him, and would often wish to be alone, or with
some other boy who would climb about, and
adventure more than Harry. Still, every morning,
when a bunch of the boys were out on the street,
he and Harry naturally joined each other, and
separated from the others to go out to this
farm.

One day the two of them watched while a mare
that had been brought out to the farm was bred,
and saw the excitement of the stallion, heard him
neigh and whisper groaningly.

« What does he do that for ? » Harry asked while
the act of breeding was going on.

« So there will be a colt. That's how young things
are always made », Harold explained.

« Not babies — not us — the doctor brings
babies », Harry said, shocked.

« Rats, that's a fairy story like Santa Claus. Men
and women do that same thing, — only a man's

thing isn't quite as big as a stallion's », Harold declared a little impatiently.

Harry was silent. A feeling of nausea and horror was numbing him inside himself.

« Don't you remember the afternoon that Tuffy Thomas came out of Casserly's barn and told you and I to go away, that he and Hazel were going to have a good time together... I knew they couldn't really — too young. You have to be grown up to be able. But Tuffy swore that he got his thing in. I don't believe him though. He likes to brag. »

Harry did not speak for sometime, until at last : « But it isn't really that way — not my mother and father, I know — they couldn't do that — I tell you what I think — they just pray and God sends a baby to them. »

« O don't be foolish. You ask Mrs. Richardson. A man puts his thing in a woman somewhere, I don't know where, and then after nine months she has a baby. You ask Tuffy, or Hazel Casserly, or any of the older fellows. It's no use asking your father and mother. They tell you fairy tales. You don't suppose it happens one way with animals and another with people, do you ? »

For days Harry could do nothing but ask questions about how babies are made. The other boys about town had their curiosity too. Whenever a group of them were together and sitting down where they could talk the conversation would turn to that subject, and each would have a theory about the act.

« I tell you I know how it's done; I've done it with Hazel », Tuffy would declare. « I'll get her and show you. »

One day, — it had rained the night before and the roads were too muddy to walk out to the farm — Harry, Tuffy, Gordon, and Harold, were playing about the barn in back of the grocery store. A rackfull of hay stood beneath the loft door, and they were turning somersets in the hay as they jumped out of the barnloft door to hay in the rack, ten feet below. After they'd been doing this for a time they all sat along the edges of the rack to get their breath, and to talk. When they had been seated there for a while Tuffy Thomas saw Hazel Casserly and Ruthie Jenkins. « Hey girls come on over, I want to ask you something », he called to them. The girls came over, and climbed up into the rack.

« These fellow don't believe that you and I did — you know what, Hazel », Tuffy said.

« Why you awful boy. I never did, and you know you said you wouldn't tell. Anyway you couldn't when you did try. Nothing happened at all », Hazel said.

« You liar! » Tuffy responded.

After some talk Hazel's indignation subsided, and Ruthie who declared she thought they were all being nasty, also began to talk, and wonder if babies really come about the way they thought they did.

« I'll tell you, let's go inside the loft, and you girls show us what you have, and we'll show you, and maybe try and see if we can make anything happen », Tuffy said at last.

« There's no use trying that. Nothing does happen until you're at least fourteen, and you don't get any feeling till then anyway. I've heard older fellows talk » Harold broke in.

Hazel and Ruth said they wouldn't think of it, and that the boys were dirty things to mention that, but after a time they weren't so sure, and finally Hazel said she would let each boy look, but one at a time, and the others would have to stand away while he was looking. So Ruthie agreed to this also.

« If I let any one of you try to do anything with me it will be Harold — or Harry — they aren't so nasty as the rest of you, but Harry's too nice a boy to want to, aren't you Harry » Ruth said.

Harry could say nothing. His heart was beating at a terrific rate. He was — not afraid — terrified rather with shame.

After they had all looked at the girls, and tried to understand how things were done Tuffy said he could demonstrate. Hazel refused, saying that she wouldn't, not with anybody, but Harold, and he said he wouldn't, not with everybody looking on, but he would try if they'd all go away and leave him and Hazel alone together, and if Harry would go on one side of the loft with Ruth, while he and Hazel were on the other side. After Harold, Hazel, Ruth and Harry, had all swore that they would tell just what happened and how it felt, the others went out, and after much exclamations and accusations, to the rest that they were peeking, Harold and Harry tried.

« I couldn't feel anything but a feeling like when your hands have gone to sleep and there's a tingle in them » Harold explained.

« We couldn't do anything at all — how can a thing go in when it's soft I don't understand » Ruth assured the others, and a little later, after explanation, asked Harold in a whisper if he'd try with her sometime, when nobody knew.

From that time on Harry seemed to care less for Harold, and wouldn't play much with him or any of the boys, but it may not have been his discovery, or the actions of that day. School had started a few days after, and his mother, saying that he'd had a free time all summer, kept him around home much, and told Harold that he'd better come up and play inside with Harry so they could get their lessons together, but Harold, not liking to be indoors and never studying anyway, would not go very often. About two weeks after school had started it rained hard one day, and Harry got his feet wet, so that a bad cold attacked him, and his throat became inflamed. He was out of school for a week. When he returned he was pale, and for the next two months coughed much, was always sickly and tired, without an interest in anything. Harold was sorry for him, and for Mrs. Wright, but he couldn't make Harry happy even by being with him, because the cough and sore throat kept him miserable all the time whether someone was with him or not.

It was three months after school started before Harry was really well again, and even then he was apathetic and lifeless. Then very suddenly he died. A case of lockjaw developed within a day, he could not speak, or move his mouth; he was in agony, and when Harold went to see him his eyes had nothing but the light of torture in them. It was a great relief when he died. It is horrible to watch somebody suffer and be able to do nothing.

« No, I'm not sorry he's dead. He never would have been wild about life if he had lived, any more than I ever will be » Harold told Tuffy Thomas, and Tuffy was shocked, saying that was no way to talk about a dead person.

The Baby of the Family

Donald came slowly down the stairs and into breakfast. He'd heard his brother's voice saying « That self–centered little brat gets down to breakfast when he wants to; he knows who's mother's pet. » Anger and bitterness were in his heart. When his brother spoke to him saying « late as usual, dear little boy » he spoke sullenly. « O keep your damn mouth shut; you tend to your own habits and I'll take care of mine. »

His sister Isabel spoke in then, remarking « Well, young man the routine of this house isn't run for your benefit; you get around to meals on time or you won't get any. »

« You're not running the household, you can bet. It's all right for you to upset everything if you want to give a party — just don't you worry so much about my bringing up. »

« Someone needs to worry. »

« It doesn't need to be you, or Lloyd; every time either of you get snubbed, or can't keep a job you try to take out your temper on all the younger members of the family ».

« Huh » sister Alice broke in « you two are just alike. The oldest and youngest, and you're both raising hell all of the time. Why don't you keep still and let things be pleasant once in a while ».

Donald looked at Alice and felt remorse within him. « You're enough older than I am not to have to fight all the time or just be made a servant; and it'd be a good thing if you would quit crying every time Isabel gets sarcastic. She can't get away with any of her nastiness on me. Don't you think I know she's mad because of last night — giving a lecture on woman suffrage and not able to hold a bonehead like Super-intendant May when he begans to ask her questions. She made some figure up there on the stage — a brilliant mind : — and then she comes around telling the rest of us how stupid we are. »

Saying this, Donald saw the he had cut Isabel, because she didn't answer back, and her face twitched a little bit. He felt sorry — a bit — and then remembering that she'd given him a dollar to spend at the Carnival last week a pang of regret struck his heart and spread. « Of course that old dub has to bring in arguments about the sanctity of the home, and bible statements that no one can contradict before a church audience without running a risk of a scandal. »

Isabel almost smiled at him, and then frowned. He understood what she felt. He supposed it was right that she and he were most alike of any two in the family, but it angered him to have her always insisting, driving, telling him and the others that they had no energy, no ambition, and permitted themselves to be patronized by other people in town, of families that had no innate culture, or intelligence. She hadn't any right to say that to him, when he knew — and was always being hurt by it — that girls and boys his age said he was a little snob who thought too much of himself. He was sick of needing to come to meals and sit without speaking while he looked sullen, and « supercilious with that big nose of his up in the air ».

« I wish to the devil that this family could get something else to talk about at meals other than me and what I do and don't do. There's one scrap around here every minute a person's in the house. It's no wonder I want go to away and stay away all day, and not come to meals at all, « he commented.

. « Why don't you get out if you don't like it ? There's many a boy not more than twelve making his own living. No one keeps you here. » Isabel said.

« You ! Who in the devil are you to advise me ? Why don't you get out yourself, you're always kicking — I guess we get on peaceably enough when you're not around, and Lloyd likes to have you think he's smart by siding in with you with your cheap criticism. You say everybody should leave their family by the time they're sixteen and you're some above that God knows. »

« You'd all live like the washerwoman's family then. Don't think I wouldn't like to get out. »

« Ho, ho, that's good. You stay here because it's cheaper than it'd be to board, and then you try to pass of the bluff that you're uplifting — no, no, don't pour out any coffee for me. I don't want any breakfast » Donald said, pushing his chair back and getting up.

« Here, here, eat your breakfast and don't act like a petty child » his mother said. « You didn't eat anything for supper last night either. »

« No. I won't eat. — You hear what's going on. Is it any wonder I hate coming down to meals ? »

« Well, well, eat you breakfast. »

« No ! — I don't see why you insist upon my not going to live with Mrs. Granger and getting my board there for work I can do. Lots of pleasure there is in keeping the family intact — Tom Mc Calaster doesn't have to listen to talk like we have all the time. »

« You should obey your elder brothers and sisters. »

« Don't make me puke. Look at them. Just why should I obey them? What have they done, who are they, what do they know — let them make something of themselves before they take on the responsibility of helping to bring me up. Obey them! Fat chance! »

« You obey me all right when I want you to »,
Lloyd said, « or you know what you get if you
don't. »

A blaze of anger was in Donald. « I do like hell.
You'd better keep some of the things you do quieter
so you don't have to come around and be nice
begging me not to tell before you brag about who
obeys you. If dad knew where you were Saturday..... »

« Keep still », Lloyd shouted out.

« You're a caddish little tattle tale » Isabel broke
in.

« I haven't told anything — but if you think I
let you and Lloyd tell me what I will or won't do,
and let you get away with it because you're strong
enough to slap me you're mistaken. I'll mind my
own business if you mind yours, and if you don't
— well, I know enough about you both to make
things uncomfortable, don't worry. »

Having said that Donald went out into the hall,
and picking up his cap pulled it down on his head
viciously. His mind was weighted with disgust; his
lungs felt smothered and his heart was heavy with
anger and resentment that had gathered within it
and grown stale.

He didn't know who to aim his resentment at,
Isabel, Lloyd, his mother, or the whole family.
Outside on the doorstep his pet cat snoozed in the
sun, and he leaned down to put his face against
its warm fur, and to talk baby talk to it. « Youse

a nice boy isn't you Ceasar; you love me Ceasar?
Yes, yes, you bet you do. »

« Go on downtown and quit acting like a two
year old with that cat. I wish he'd scratch your
face off », Lloyd called out to him, and Donald
leaped back embarrassed, ashamed of being
caught talking to the cat. Then he picked up Ceasar and went down the path to the gate, and
cuddled it after he got outside and was going down
the path past the orchard to the main road leading
downtown. At the corner of the orchard he sat
down in the grass with Ceasar in his lap, leaning
his face down to him to whisper in his furry
ear. When Ceasar began to purr, and to reach
his nose up to touch Donald's and indicated
that he wanted to be stroked, Donald grew more
affectionate still. He didn't feel so bitter now;
scenes like the one past were too frequent so he
forgot them at once. But a helpless, hopeless, des-
pondency was settling into him. He wanted to cry
but defiance would not let him. He regretted not
having let Lloyd's first remark go by and then he
could have eaten silently, and looked distant if
they'd talked about him, because wrangles like
that never get anywhere. He remembered that it
was Saturday and that he'd told Tommie Mc Calaster that he'd go out to the lake to swim with him;
but now he could not because he had no money to
rent a bathing suit and couldn't go back to the
house and ask anybody for fifty cents. Isabel

would probably be the only one who had it anyway.

He was feeling much misused by life. As he sat there he began to tell himself a story of which he was the hero, some years further on, when Isabel and Lloyd, and all the others were wanting his help because he was a great man, acclaimed by the whole world, — and he was kind to them, but he had to be a little ironical in his kindness, to tantalize them as they had tantalized him. Upon recalling that Mr. Layman had told his mother that Donald was the happiest boy he'd ever known, and was always whistling and singing whenever he came out to his farm to work for a few days, a great wave of melancholy and self-pity swept over him. He, a happy boy — how little Mr. Layman understood. He could whistle and sing out in the country, all right. He liked feeding the calves and petting them, and putting his face up against theirs; and he liked milking Mr. Layman's registered Jersey cows, knowing that some of the most beautiful ones of them were friendly to him and caressed him as they never would Mr. Layman. But that didn't make him a happy boy for other times. If it weren't for his little pet pig, and Ceasar and Tommie Mc Calaster he'd be so unhappy he couldn't live.

« O here's Donnie », a voice said, and he looked up to see Mrs. Farmer with another lady he didn't know. « I'm just going to see if your mother won't bake a cake for the Methodist social tonight — as it's for charity even if she is a Presbyterian. »

« Yes, Mrs. Farmer » Donnie said, and wished she would hurry on and leave him to talk on to himself.

« Perhaps you can run and tell her and save me the walk », Mrs. Farmer added.

« It wouldn't do any good. I've just had a scrap with the whole family, » Donald said.

Mrs. Farmer laughed, and said « Well, it's not far. I'll ask her myself. This is Mrs. Todd, who has a boy just your age and they will live in town from now on ». Then she spoke to Mrs. Todd « You must have your boy come and see Donnie. They must be friends. Donnie is such a sophisticated boy. Really. » — She said in a lower voice « I've never seen a boy so mature for his age. He carries on a conversation like a grown man. » Then she went on down the path towards the house.

Donald's eyes followed her coldly, and his melancholy hardened into disdainful bitterness for a moment, while he reflected how little good it did for him to be sophisticated. But his vanity was pleased, and in a minute or so he put Ceasar down, realizing that such pursuits as talking lovetalk to a cat are not for a boy so mature-minded as he was. Striding off down town he looked as nonchalant and as indifferent to any interests that might be called childish as possible. He was quite happy, congratulating himself on how well he could hold his own in an argument with Isabel to keep her from bossing him. Almost a tenderness for Isabel arose up in him because she permitted him to demonstrate his ability, and also he recalled how sometimes she would, in an affectionate mood, hug and kiss him, and give him money very frequently. O he understood Isabel. He was proud of her too because everybody spoke of her style, her wit, her brilliant conversation — with anybody not in the family, and no one is going to waste brilliant conversation on a member of their own family. He liked walking downtown with her, and was as conscious as she was that other women looked enviously at her clothes, which she wore with so much dignity, poise, and vivacious style of manner. Such times Donald felt that he was almost wearing Isabel as an ornament to himself — or that she wore him — nobody ever attracted more admiring attention than the two of them, when Isabel was along. Maybe she wasn't pretty — prettiness is a silly quality. She was dignified, and she had an intelligent face. He felt almost friendly enough towards her now to go back and ask her for fifty cents, but he knew that would be no use unless Mrs. Farmer had stayed to talk, because Isabel probably wouldn't be in a friendly mood yet, but if Mrs. Farmer was there he could say something that would make them all laugh, andd then confide in front of them all that he wanted fifty cents.

Upon reflection however he grew a little bitter and angry at Isabel, and wouldn't take the chance of going back. That would simply allow her to say that he was always sponging on her when another quarrel came up. He would never, never, ask her for money, and he would refuse it if she offered it to him. Having so decided he went on to Tommie's house and whistled outside it till Tommie appeared.

« I can't go swimming; don't you go either. The water won't be any good today. Come on and we'll go down to the crick and see if we can catch some frogs; then we can have some fried frog legs. I'm hungry; had a fight at breakfast time and cleared out before I'd eaten anything », he told Tommie.

« No siree, I'm going swimming. Pete has money. You never have any ». Tommie said curtly, and Donald looked at him surprised, since Tommie before had always stayed with him in preference to Pete. He was hurt.

« Go ahead then. Lot I care. You and Pete are about the same rate anyway ; afraid of getting your feet wet if you go frogging » he answered and walked away. He wouldn't turn around or pay any attention to Tommie when he called out to him. Broodingly he decided to walk out to Mr. Layman's farm to see if any new calves had been born yet. Mr. Layman had said about a week ago that the little heiffer, Bianca, only fourteen months old, was to calve soon. Her calf would have to be a tiny tike, and hoping that it had arrived caused him to become cheerful, so that as he walked along he felt exhuberant and sang to himself until he was well on the outskirts of town. Then he began singing in as loud a voice as he could, and was vain within himself that he knew so many songs from Grand Opera. As he sang he imagined an audience listening him, awestruck with the volume and beauty of his voice. The audience was made up of magnificently dressed ladies and gentlemen, all of them either famous themselves or beautiful to look at· They were astounded with wonder when, besides, singing, he danced for them, and danced better than any Russian dancer had ever danced. As he ran for a spurt, and leapt into the hair whirling around, and doing steps to waltz music, he felt marvellously conquering, and could imagine the long applause which his singing and dancing drew from the awestruck multitudes. For a time after a buggy passed him he walked stiffly, afraid that the farmer in the buggy had seen him jumping around and would think him silly. But that fear passed, and he began singing to himself again as loud as he could, except that he kept a watchout around him to be sure that no buggy, or nobody came upon him unawares to catch him acting his romantic stories to himself, because he knew that it isn't sophisticated or mature to act dreams out like that.

Mr. Layman wasn't at the farm, but his wife was,

and she said her husband was out in the field, but surely Donald knew where the calves were kept by now. « You'll have to be careful with Bianca though. The little thing is ferocious now that she has a.calf, and she's won't have it frightened. »

« O Bianca knows me; she'll let me play with her calf », Donald boasted, and went out to the shed. Bianca was there and her calf was not half the size of ordinary jersey calves which are small at their largest. No bigger than a fair sized cat was it. Bianca tossed her head, and lowed menacingly. Donald was afraid to get in the pen with her at first, but finally after having given her a handfull of hay, and petted her head, he saw that she had only been fooling him and wasn't afraid at all that he'd hurt her baby. So he climbed in, and petted Bianca, until she began to rub her head against his shoulders as she always did before. But the calf trotted away when he tried to touch it — very lively — and it kicked up its back heels, ran under Bianca's belly.

When he caught hold of it to pet it, Bianca looked dubiously cross. The calf tried to get away at first but calmed down in about a minute while Donald leaned down to stroke its face, and look into its liquid luminous eyes. So he stayed to pet the calf and Bianca, and talk to them for almost an hour. He assured Bianca and the calf — a bull calf — that he'd see to it that no butcher came to get this calf. He'd make Mr. Layman let it be one to raise for a breed bull, both of them need not fear, because he was afraid that Mr. Layman would think the calf born of too young a mother to ever make a good service bull. It wasn't a nice idea to think that so tiny a thing would be taken away by the butcher.

Within an hour though he heard Mrs. Layman calling to him and ran out, because he knew that it was dinner time and that she was going to ask him to stay and eat with them.

« You'll have to own a stockfarm of your own someday sure, won't you Donnie », Mr. Layman said at the dinner table. « I guess I'll see if I can't adopt you, to have you help with the chores around the farm here. »

Donald said nothing, but felt skeptical about that, because chores around a farm mean much work and even feeding the calves and caring for them is a messy job if you get too much of it. He did not state his misgiving though, for he knew the adoption idea was only a passing fancy to Mr. Layman, if his mother would permit it.

All afternoon Donald played around the farm, by the stacks of alfalfa hay, out in the cow pasture, in the orchard looking for birds' nests.

Down at the pig barn he sat on the railing for a half an hour to watch one of the sows that was giving birth to a litter of pigs. When he arrived already six pigs had been born, and as he watched, five more came, so he knew that was a big litter. It startled him every time a little pig was born, because they popped out so unexpectedly. He didn't dare get in the pen with the sow though, to pick up one of the pink-nosed porkers for fear she'd take a chunk out of his leg.

By the time five o'clock came he concluded he'd better start back to town to be able to loiter on the way if he saw reason to. The cattle were all coming slowly up from the meadow, where they browsed and stood in the swamp during the heat of the day. He called out their names, and two of them came over to the fence to sniff him and to be petted; even Silver King, the bull, who was nasty tempered generally, stood placidly at the fence and put his glistening nose to the wires. He did not draw back his head when Donald put a hand to the side of his jowl to pat him.

A gentle sweet melancholy permeated all of Donald's being; beneath all his tranquil contemplation a vague, desolating unrest abided, but calm was uppermost in his spirit for the now. As he walked off down the road he told himself that a simple life on the farm was the life to live; that he must have no ambitions to gain the acclaim of people — which is futile recognition — he must no longer desire to be brilliant, and defiant, and combative — to fight on towards some end which he desired without knowing what that end was.

Yet he realized vaguely too, that such life could never satisfy him; that he tired of petting the

6

calves, of talking to the animals — and he did not talk to them, except of himself generally — they, just as the cat, were simply live ears into which he could say aloud his dreams and hopes. A sense of guilt arose in him as he thought of Bianca's calf, and realized that he wouldn't actually care if the butcher did come to take it away. It was only in moments of thinking it darling and cute looking, while petting it and liking the warm affection-inspiring touch of its small face against his own that the thought of its not being any more to touch hurt him. Life — something it had in common with himself — made him care for it, but nevertheless it was only himself he was really caring about. He wondered if he did, or if he ever would, love anybody, or anything; if he even loved himself.

He tried to think and decide what to think of life, but he came to no clear conclusion.

Three Girls

Besides being so beautiful that the memory of them brings up in one's mind, a young boy when he last saw them, their faces when the word beauty is spoken, Myrtle Rose and Fay Townsend had also proved to have voices that were surely meant to be heard by admiring multitudes. It is hard to think of loveliness such as theirs as allowed to fade in a small village, since people who knew them, young boys particularly, must have thought of the beauty of goddesses and fabled ladies of antiquity, in terms of Fay and Myrtle.

Fay certainly belonged upon the stage, because her walk, the carriage of her head upon a slender neck in a leading fashion, made onlookers conscious that she was conscious of beauty. Viewed closely, she seemed un-actual, not to be touched or spoken to. Her orange gold eyes, her moongleaming chestnut hair, the bright alway blushing pinkness of her glowing skin, made her rather a picture, or a dream, than a real girl.

On Sundays Leila Mackaye had used to sing in the church choir, and a very sweet well-trained voice she had, with indications of dramatic power — but hymn singing in a presbyterian church permits these indications to flower little. The night however, that Myrtle Rose and Fay Town-send sang the solos parts in Handel's Easter Oratorio so brilliantly that they moved the audience more than David Tolls, whom critics had said was to be one of the great tenors of the day, Leila Mackaye stood at the back of the church looking and listening. It was generally said that Leila took arsenic in a much diluted form to add to her pallor, but whether that be so or not, her face was magnesium white, with a bloodless whiteness intensified by the ashen blackness of her hair, and the staring blackness of her eyes. Standing there she looked tired, apathetic, indif-ferent to life, and a simple black satin dress she wore clung to her lithe body in tired folds. It was hard for some people to know where to look, at Myrtle, at Fay, or at Leila — beneath the tiredness though of Leila there seemed most power for some reason. But after this night Leila would sing no more in the church choir. « What is the use », she asked, « where could I ever get with my voice and looks if a town this size produces two girls so breathlessly beautiful who can sing naturally better than I do after three years training? The cities must have innumerable others. »

There had always been unspoken, but understood, scandal about Leila — the dubious origin of her, the strange family circumstance, her indifferent readiness to go out on a night with worthless men, had caused this to be. She lived with Mr. and Mrs. Drayman. Mr. Drayman was the wealthiest man in town, a banker well past fifty, with dull eyes, a reckless contempt of people and still some romanticism in him — there must have been; for he had married « that » woman — other women said she had been a mistress of a house of ill fame — they said — well it was what they restrained themselves from saying because whatever she had been she was the wife of a wealthy man, lived in a magnificent mansion, gave musicals, entertained nobility from Europe, with whom she had herself photographed to let the papers reproduce the pictures. Mrs. Drayman's dimensions should have saved her from the breath of scandal now, because in a photograph of her beaded « Mrs. Drayman in a hunting suit in Switzerland. The men are the Duke of — and Count — respectively well known members of the English and French nobility », and Mrs. Drayman's circumference was over twice that of both the Duke and the Count put together. Nevertheless she had been a handsome woman; she was yet; her violet eyes were still violet; her massive face still had a greeklike profile, severe in the profile, and dolllike from the front view. It was not known what relation Leila was to either Mr. or Mrs.

Drayman, or whether they had simply adopted her. When Mrs. Drayman came into church on a Sunday morning — and it was the only social function she attended except the great entertaiments she herself gave — there was a stir. There needed to be; her commanding size clad in bright-hued dresses of expensive embroidery, or light stuffs in the summer months, with picture hats, chiffon hats, tiny cuddling hats, above them, demanded a stir. She, and Leila, and Mr. Drayman came in at different times, and seemed indifferent to each other, though it was known that they all got on most amiably together, Mr. Drayman permitting both of the women utmost freedom.

People were a trifle surprised when Fay and Myrtle began to go around together, and surprised when Leila joined them in friendship, because all three girls had always kept themselves aloof from other girls, and all had a glamour about them that no girl in town had ever had before. O Myrtle was more approachable than the other two. Till she was fifteen Myrtle had been in the gradeschool without being able to pass into the eighth grade; and other girls said she was thick-headed. She was a good-natured being; during the winter months for several years she had gone with her parents to stay in California, or to cruise down around Florida. Coming home in the spring she would bring back colored sands, shell fish, coral, and would talk for the class, telling them of trips in glass-bot-

tomed boats, through which one can see coloured
jelly fishes, sea vegetation, and other wonders of
the deep. When she was sixteen though she quit
school for good ; her mind was not a scholastic one ;
and a year later, returning from Europe, she
astounded everybody by being more beautiful than
Fay Townsend. Dressed in a tailored suit, she
would swing down the main street with an athletic
stride, her broad shoulders giving to her a handsome swagger that Fay could not equal. Her manner
was direct and simple ; if she heard that someone
thought her « the most beautiful girl he's ever
seen » she would remark « well what of it ; don't
blame me. » She accepted the adoration of young
men in town humourously ; and when older men,
bachelors of wealth who were generally afraid of
matrimonially inclined young ladies, were frank
in their desire to woo her, Myrtle accepted their
attentions with phlegmatic whimsicality. If a young
man had declared that he was going to call on Fay
Townsend other young men would have doubted
him, and wondered how he managed it ; not so with
Myrtle. She'd sit out on the front porch of her house
and say « hello » to people passing, and if they'd
stop to talk, invite them to come and sit on the
steps. Often quite a group of young men would be
dangling over the railings of her front porch. But of
course it was expected the Myrtle would marry
some very wealthy man from away.

All of the girls were about eighteen when it was

discovered, first that Fay had a marvelous soprano voice, and then that Rose had one as marvelous, and not so theatrical, with more emotional quality in it. After taking lessons with David Tolls for six months, Fay sang one night at a musical, and sang the waltz song from *Romeo and Juliet* so that she made people gasp with wonder. « She'll be one of the great singers of the world — and with her looks » : they stood around saying afterwards. There was brilliance, volume, exuberance, lilt — her voice was glorious, young and healthy. Then Myrtle Rose came out to sing. Her immediate effect was not so electric, because she was dressed more simply, and did not come with such a sweeping manner unto the stage. But during the course of time, while she was singing a group of old English songs, people began to feel that Fay had too much artificiality about her methods to have the mighty appeal of this girl, who without the slightest effort at brilliance or at volume, filled the auditorium with perfectly toned music. « Miss Townsend is a brilliant singing machine ; Miss Rose interprets her songs and has quite as glorious a voice, of greater warmth », the paper said next day.

Leila Mackaye had refused to sing.

Nobody could interest Myrtle Rose in a career. « What's the use. I won't be any happier that way — it's a struggle. You can't walk into glory », she declared. Within a year she had married a nice young man from a neighboring town, and became domestic. She said she loved him, and didn't care much about other people. She was happy.

Fay Townsend went to Minneapolis to have her voice trained for going upon the concert stage as soon as possible, to go into grand opera later probably. Within a year she was back and evaded singing, and soon married Jake Corneliuson, a white-headed young fellow whose father had money so saw that he kept a position in some bank. It was understood that in Minneapolis they had been so enthusiastic about Fay that they overtrained her voice, and in straining it, made it necessary for her not to use it for a year at least. Fay evidently decided that the road to fame was too rocky. Within three years her slender neck was fleshier, as was her face, so that her gold-orange eyes seemed embedded a bit too much in flesh. She would always be beautiful, and would perhaps make as lovely an elderly lady as her mother, but the lustre of her loveliness was gone.

But Leila Mackaye was still about town, unmarried, and going about alone since Myrtle and Fay had been away, married, and forgotten apparently their one summer friendship with her. She had ceased singing entirely. Sometimes she would be gone from town for several months, staying in some city — it was not known where. She cared for no one apparently, would appear on the streets sometimes, always modishly dressed, but when Mrs. Drayman entertained, Leila either did not

come down stairs, or just strolled in for a few
minutes and went upstairs again. Mrs. Drayman
said one time to a clever, vivacious young school-
teacher who had come to teach in the highschool,
« O I am bored, bored with living. If you play the
piano or sing you can come and live with me and
I'll give you all the money you want, give you
these pictures stuck around here on the wall, give
you all the clothes you want. I do wish I could
find somebody who played the piano magnificently
who would stay here and play for me when I want
to hear music, and I love music. » But Mrs. Drayman didn't mention Leila, or criticize her, except
that one time when an over-inquisitive lady spoke
saying : « I suppose you're much disappointed that
you daughter didn't go on with her music »,
trying thereby to get Mrs. Drayman to say whether
or not Leila was her daughter, Mrs. Drayman answered: « My daughter — O you mean Leila — well,
no, yes — no, no, — she's what she is. I understand a person wanting to be and do as she does
want to be or do. »

There seemed now to be a little contempt in
Leila's manner for Fay — Corneliuson — whose
beauty having diluted, had neither much wit or
energy, but who still retained a nonchalantly con-
sciously-beautiful manner.When Myrtle Rose came
to visit town with her young husband Leila was
friendly with her, because her husband was a
charming boy, and Myrtle was still the simple,

good-natured person she'd always been and was quite as lovely as ever in a more feminine way since her baby had been born.

Around the Drayman mansion was a hedge of evergreen stubs; within their enclosure were two acres of land planted with bushes, pod plants, trees, and most of all with lilac bushes. Perhaps it was the numerous lilac bushes that caused Leila to give one young boy an impression always of lilacs, for surely in her dead whiteness, and in the ash-blackness of her hair, the blind-staring blackness of her eyes, was no lilac colour. Beneath the whiteness of her skin — of course there was colour in her blood, the blackness of her eyes must have been a composition of colours to attain that blackness. Perhaps the faint perfume she wore was lilac perfume.

It was spring. About the Drayman mansion two hundred lilac bushes were abloom, so that the scent of the flowers carried for at least a mile, a lavender vapour hovered about the land in their vicinity on evenings; a dazzle of prismatic colour tingled and vibrated in the air nearby during the sunshine hours, a mist of glowing colour without a mist of vapours. One night Leila could have been seen standing erect by one of the lilac bushes, her pale face lifted up, her white neck showing slenderly against a cluster of lilacs, her eyelids half closed. There was desolation and tragic nunlike beauty about her figure. A sense came to one that

a torrent had passed, a battle had raged, as she
stood there — a widow of passion. Why her quietness gave an impression of intensity I do not know.
It may have been true that she had loved Denton
Manners, a reckless dissolute fellow, who after
going with her a time had eloped with a telephone
girl; perhaps her apathy tired him.

For the week there was at the town hall a travelling hypnotist, who already had made several
weak sort of young men perform ridiculous things
on the stage after they'd swaggered up declaring
that he couldn't hypnotize them. Of course the
hypnotist was a striking looking man, sinister, in
a way, mysterious. Hypnotism is hard to explain
or to understand. His eyes had a fascination about
them. Very large they were, and of a colour hard
to discover — black, dark blue, or violet, or brown,
or black. His face was thin; his lips — sensitive
thin lips, but hard with a subtle cruelty. He was a
charlatan of course, and when he failed to hypnotize a person — particularly the night he failed to
hypnotize two twelve year old boys — he would
make a remark such as « The subject must have a
mind — a mind — that is a mind that can concentrate, you know » and a ripple of laughter would
run through the auditorium. It was generally
believed that he couldn't hypnotize anybody but
a weak-willed person, for certainly of the six men
he'd hypnotized there was not one who had any
will to speak of. Having hypnotized Bill McKinnon

eight times, it was little wonder that he could concentrate and make Bill come up on the stage from away back in the hall — or even draw him from home perhaps. When it was advertised that he would put a lady to sleep, and have her placed in a show window on the main street where she would sleep without stirring or seeming to breathe for twentyfour hours, there was general skepticism. It was said that twice during the twenty-four hours, the hypnotist, remaining in his room at the hotel, would cause the lady to turn over.

Several ladies and men in town wondered if they had not better send a telegram to Mr. and Mrs. Drayman who were in the city for a week, when it was discovered that Leila Mackaye was going to submit herself to the test. Particularly did they think it was necessary to do this 'after Leila had clearly been hypnotized twice, up on the 'stage.

« I don't believe it ; I don't think he had the girl hypnotized. She is infatuated with him and will do whatever he wants her to » Attorney Porter declared. « The girl is only unhappy, and his unusual personality fascinates her. One look at her and anyone could know that she's the type of person given to moods of desperation. »

Nobody however telegraphed to Mr. or Mrs. Drayman, and one day Leila was placed, hypnotized, on a cot in a show–window of an empty store building. Her body was straightened out, and lay motionless, on its back. It looked like an uncoloued

wax figure. Her hair looked as though it were a
wig not made of human hair, and seemed simply
resting upon her skull. If she were shamming, she
shammed perfectly; or she was drugged. There
was not a motion or a quiver upon any muscle of
her body that watching eyes could detect. People
were not positive whether she turned over at the
hours set or not because such a jam was around
the window, shoving to look at her, and there was
so much argument and assertion and denial that
people near the window said they weren't sure
whether they saw her turn over or not. They
seemed to have hypnotized themselves.

That point remained unsettled, but she rested
there on the cot for twenty-four hours. A week
after that day, when the hypnotist left town
she too left town. Reports came back that she was
permitting herself to be hypnotized on the stage,
and to be made to sleep the twenty-four hour
sleep, in every town at which the hypnotist stopped
to give his show. Other reports came back that
she had left the hypnotist, and was working as
a stenographer in Sioux Falls, the novelty and
exotic quality of the man having ceased to be
novel or exotic for her once she knew him inti-
mately. « She wouldn't permit him to dominate
her for long », her defenders argued.

Within six months Leila was back in town, and
said nothing of where she had been or what she
had been doing, unless it was to the Draymans

who made no practice of explaining things to
fellow townspeople. Leila was a little thinner, a
little more unaware of reality in her manner, detached and indifferent. There was no proof of the
gossip which said she'd been operated on to avoid
having a baby. The scandal about her was yet large-
ly unspoken scandal, a sort of « Leila Mackaye
— O yes, yes — ah ha — I wonder » mention of
her, with no more definite comment.

She did not marry. She went from town and
remained away for intervals of months at a time,
and no one knew where unless it was the Draymans. When in town she appeared on the streets
seldom, and spoke abstractedly to passers by she
knew. Going by the Drayman estate one might see
her sometimes sitting on the lawn, reading, or
moving about amongst the bushes, perhaps picking
a rose, or leaning to smell some flower growing on
a bush or plant. At evening, during springtime
when the lilacs were abloom she could be seen
strolling about the lawn of an evening, for the
evening air, to rub the softness of the gentle atmosphere into her spirit, perhaps. Many a time she
stood erect by one of the lilac bushes, her pale face
lifted up, her slender neck cut like a cameo against
a cluster of lilac flowers and lilac leaves, her eyelids
closed. There was always intense quietness about
her then, desolation, as though some dumb doubt
and wonder had ravaged her.

« Leila is a weak sort of girl », Fay Corneliuson

would say of her, and look at her a little enviously, for by now Fay could appear before people and cause no ripple of admiration, but Leila's pale face always would make her a striking personality; a quality within her always gave one a feeling of power.

« Fay had better say nothing of Leila's weakness », Myrtle Rose would say. « She doesn't understand what she's talking about. Leila wasn't meant to be a housewife like Fay and myself. She makes me want to cry — I do wish I could help her, but I don't understand. »

« One of us should have had a career Myrtle, you, or Fay, or I. You at least though are beautiful, yet. How can Fay be complacent about herself now, having been so lovely and had so much promise. O, one of the three of us should have gone beyond this — anybody can live as we live. »

Once in a great while piano playing could be heard to some from the Drayman house, and a contralto voice of great power would send vibrations of intense music pressingly through the atmosphere. At these times anybody who heard must stand stark still to listen, for the voice swept aside material purposes and ideas and left in the hearer only an emotion of pent-up tragedy, exalted reverence, and an emotion of longing caught and held static at its highest pitch.

But these times were rare, and Leila Mackaye would never sing in public. People were afraid to ask her to any longer.

Filling the Pulpit

Three ministers to the pulpit of the Presbyterian Church had come and gone since the departing of the Reverend G. Ogden Robinson. Mrs. Davis, who, however much of a rake her husband might be, was a quiet, gentile, church-going lady, was heard to regret frequently that the Rev. Robinson had felt urged to answer the call from another fold.

Indeed she had never quite approved of his playing tennis, and he had taken rather too youthful an interest in owning a fine-appearing horse to drive about in paying parish calls, and these things she doubted were quite seemly for a minister of the gospel and a father of an eighteen year old daughter. It was not to be disputed however that the Rev. Robinson presented a distinguished person in group gatherings of churchmen, being both tall, erect, and while lithe, very sedate of bearing. He was also a well read man. Every book that Mrs. Davis could mention to him he knew, and many others besides.

He had heard the call however; and the last three ministers had both been found unsatisfactory by, and had found, unsatisfactory, the community of Merivale. Mrs. Davis had few interests in life other than church interests. Quietly she managed her household, the greatest one in town; quietly she came down to breakfast in the morning, and if Mr. Davis were not off in the city on one of his rakish expeditions, quietly she conversed with him. There was an ethereal pallor about the lady; blue veins around her eyes; patience and submission in her manner. Indeed, she would never be a woman to go so far against the word of God as to seek a divorce, whatever errors her spouse commited. Her daughter, Ethel, too, was quiet, distinguished of bearing, with always the aristocratic charm of quiet dignity about her.

Now, the fourth minister since the Rev. Robinson, had been occupying the pulpit for three Sundays. The first Sunday everybody had been pleased with his sermon, with his manner of delivery, with his healthy, manly appearance.

Even Mrs. Davis was not sure but what he, the Rev. Woollan, would prove satisfactory. It was not until she saw him driving in a buggy, and driving such a horse as Rev. Robinson had never driven that she had misgivings. Actually, he drove like an experienced horseman. The mare he drove was restive, long-bodied, slender, trim-ankled, bright-eyed, with a head that tossed about nervously, and a frame that was aquiver with restlessness as she danced about.

When Rev. Woolan stopped upon seeing her just turning the walk up to her house, and, lifting his hat, greeted her, Mrs. Davis, greeted him graciously, and came to the curbing to exchange courtesies. She liked his manner of rather brusque, awkward gallantry. Experience with Mr. Davis had taught her not to be too admiring of suavity in men.

« Quite a nice pet of a mare I have, ain't it » the Rev. Woollan commented, after an exchange of weather and health remarks. « I always like to have such a one on hand; my hobby; keeps the mind fresh. This one can do a mile in considerable under two minutes. »

That remark sealed the Rev. Woollan's doom in the community.

« It seems hardly the correct thing for a minister of the word of God to be interested in horse-racing; and to be boasting of it », Mrs. Davis was saying to Mrs. Hart not fifteen minutes after the Rev. Woollan had tipped his hat and driven away. At the time she had intended going into her house to start preparations for supper. However she postponed preparations long enough to call on a few near neighbors and tell them that she feared, that after all their hopefulnnes regarding the new minister, he was not the man for their pulpit.

« The man does not use proper English. In the course of a minute, while uttering not more than three sentences, surely not more than three, he used « ain't » twice. There's a quaint provincial tang to his method of speaking — where did the man come from originally, I wonder. I am positive that he can't be college bred ; at least that his origin is decidedly common. »

Two weeks later when Mrs. Davis heard that the Rev. Woollan had sent his horse — the Rev. Robinson never, never would have lapsed into the vulgarity of using such terms as « mare » to a lady — to the Fair grounds stable to be trained for entry into the fall races, Mrs. Davis was, she was, appaied.

In the meantime Mrs. Woollan had arrived in town, and was now settled at the parsonage. Many ladies in town were rather impressed by Mrs Woollan, who had distinct style as regards dress. Evidently she had money in her own name to be able to own a sealskin coat, and a beaverskin hat, and such gowns as she wore. She was a large, quiet-voiced woman, with a drawl in her contralto way of speaking, and generally wore dresses of clinging satin about the house. A decidedly handsome woman she was in a dusky way, with soft chestnut hued hair and deep grey eyes.

It was Mrs. Davis who first noticed that she too used the word « ain't » in speaking, and had other oddities of speach.

« O yes, a nice woman in her way », Mrs. Davis said, « but hardly an upper class way, you know. She is kind-hearted, I am sure...So also is my washerwoman. »

It was evident that both the Reverend and his

wife desired much to get on in this new parish; in
which case, Mrs. Davis believed, it would have
been better for Mrs. Woollan not to have called on
so many ladies in the community, since the manner of a social inferior would creep into her
method of talking to them.

The ruddy, windblown redness of the Reverend's
cheeks, the blocky, stalwart build of his body, the
abrupt decisive mode of his walk, became subjects
for conversation amongst tea ladies of the presbyterian congregation, each one noting this or that
little indication of vulgar origin in the gentleman's
make-up.

In consequence of which a coolness of manner
was in the treatment of Mrs. Woollan by most of
the ladies, so that she came to pay little attention
to the social duties of a minister's wife, and seemed
quietly hurt, and sensitive about speaking, as
though aware of comments that had been made
about her dialect.

However, because of the rapid change of ministers in Merivale, it was deemed hardly advisable to
immediately request another new minister, and
thus earn a name as a congregation not to be satisfied. But when Mrs. Davis discovered that the Rev.
Woollan had taken an order for a piano from
Mrs. Dolgran, and had told that lady that he was
accustomed to solving the problem of living on a
minister's salary by selling pianos, Rev. Woollan's
days were numbered.

« Indeed he has more the manner of a piano agent — of a house peddlar in fact — than of a minister. I cannot tolerate this; not and remain an active member of the First Presbyterian Church » she spoke, and having spoken, she spoke more. A meeting of the church officials was called; several meetings were held and one sunshiny morning in the early spring the Reverend Woollan delivered his sermon, a short one, and at the end stated that he would deliver no more sermons from this pulpit. It was not the correct procedure. He should have tendered a resignation; should have appreciated the dignity of his office and have been much less casual and jovially indifferent about the matter. But there the congregation was — without a minister to deliver them their sermons for three months or more, since the district assembly seemed in no hurry to rush another deliverer of the gospel word to their pulpit. Nevertheless it was not without relief that Mrs. Davis, and some others, heard the abrupt verdict.

« I understand that he has said he will give up the ministry and go into business; as a piano agent he should succeed I am sure », Mrs. Davis said to ladies she was conversing with after the church service.

But Mrs. Davis did not think that he would go into business in Merivale, and that a business of piano selling in a shop rented from her own husband, who had signed a contract for a year's lease before she knew what he was about.

And she did not think that capping such bad taste, the now Mr. Woollan and his wife, would attend the First Presbyterian church regularly when a new minister had been procured, and in coming and going quite ignore her own presence. It was an easy matter, however, to see that they did this out of bravado, for Mr. Woollan's red face would be flushed a deeper red, and Mrs. Woollan's lips could be seen to tremble while she fussed with her gloves and hands during the ceremony; and in coming into and going out of the church their slow walk was always self-conscious.

The American Critic

L. B. Squirt would never permit his Hebraic
taste for the gorgeous and spicedly sensual more
than an inhibited existence. In someway the
alchemy of an almost Bostonian « best people »
reserve had eaten its way into his blood. He could
not, however, rest upon such superior disdainings,
since some mighty inner impulse to belong was
forever preventing his ability for silent contempt
to function. An insistently young, carefree jaunt
through the French provinces, contact with such
surface brilliances as Paris in the past permitted
the clever but unsponsored foreigner, and continual companionship with Bulger, had also played
havoc with his acquired reserve.

There were few times in his life when Squirt
was not a mail philanderer, as well as desirous of
having actual affairs with women of chic and
charm. Some unkind trick of nature, though, had
made him unprepossessing, with no innate consciousness of wit, if not of intellect, to save his
hauteur from being the obvious mask which

obsequious souled people will assume. In his later
years, at the height of his public acclaim, when
discerning people would remark : « the public has
caught up to Squirt, so naturally he is popular.
Soon it will be past adoring his obvious flavours »,
he might pass forty men and give them all the
snub supreme, but some keener forty first would
sense the grovel in his snobbery, so that sniff the
rare ethers which only a nose literarily aloft can
sniff as he might he gave no impression of conscious superiority.

It was in England, where some unsigning
reviewer is forever displaying myopic insight into
the soul of America, that Squirt was dubbed the
most American of critics. The praise came at a
time when it was no longer his buoyant joy to
frenetically search for a yankee vocabulary with
the weedlike tang of his country where intellects
are trained to eat only out of the hands of economic grandeur. Tiredness of the mind, of the
spirit, and more particularly of the body — he
being of the race that yearns early in life for
definite personal security, home life, comfort and
recognition that need not be fought for to retain
— was,winding its gelatinous tenacles about him.

To him came no realization that much cleverness
is only a manifestation of insentiency, evasive of
issues and self-proclamatory. He did, however,
sense that words and ideas, however much their
journalese has been transcendentalized, but which

cut no deeper than obvious peculiarities, do not constitute evidence of understanding. He sensed, also, since the intuitions of even « smart » people are more or less honest, that one does not penetrate sensitive evaluations with ideational writing. So his acclaim of poets with the wind–yodel of the prairies and the hog–man stench of Chicago in their rhythms, came to lack vigour, since middle age was robbing him of his own gusto.

His premonitions of his own obsolescence were increased by the fact that the « game of writing » — to him — had passed the stage in his country where tracking a metaphor to its lair, to toussle it, puppy like, unaware that in spite of its apparent magnitude the brute is without real weight, causes a man to be called a poet. The smart men of his day, who made a profession of writing because of financial seduction, and who brought great aptitude for sure–fire humour and not–too–delicate analysis, he discovered to be no longer deemed smart, and none of the writers of élite mentalities were submitting material to his clever monthly for publication.

That point of «smartness» was indeed the literary death blow to Squirt. After many years, he could hardly make himself realize that interest in the erotic situation, the glibly sophisticated, the pun, the gay risque world, was no longer a fashionable interest. Truly, the smart people of this later day were wearing minds that were « intellectually

honest », given to recognizing the spiritual pauper-
ism of this their country, and addicted to spiritual hunger which dug deep roots into economic
unrest, so that no chic mentality could desire
anything less of life than complete social reorga-
nization.

Squirt could not quite bring himself to appre-
ciating the newer fashions in perceiving; though
he relaxed so far as to accept revolutionary verse
such as dealt however with staid and tried themes,
on memory, on death, on contemplation of the
infinities in a girls boarding-school manner. He
could be heard frequently to prophecy a « reaction
back to the classics », and would when speaking
critically, mention ladies who formed the American
Triumvirate of Great Woman Poets, or men who
had soil depth to them.

Passé though Squirt might be, his days of mail
philandering were not over. From the past arose
phantoms. This or that lady of literary promise,
who had forsaken the call for a few years to
become a wife and a mother, would, after a time,
recall that Squirt had encouraged her in her aspir-
ations. Forthwith, between household duties, the
movies, lectures on the social revolution, and adjust-
ing the baby's intimacies, she would sit down and
write « just a simple little thing », and in the
exhuberance of her rejuvensecence would also pen
a zestful, flirt–witty note to L. B. In the course of a
few days, since he accepted Ms. quickly, she would

receive his « Hail old mail flame » and an acceptance check with — as reminiscence sometimes
brings a glow — a remnant of his old fervour and
fever for words and phrases in the accompanying
note.

But such events were of passing satisfaction to
L. B. Squirt, since the smart people of his day did
not know of his magazine except to have vague
notions that it had ceased publication. Always
disdainful of the popular mentality, unaware
of the calm type which does not require assertive
judgments, L. B. was tiredly conscious that he was
not changing with the change of the times.

And Bulger, his colleague, always flippantly the
stronger will, and also always the echo, the crusad-
ing critic armed with glibness — well, there was
a college instructor in a course in Journalism out
in a small Western university who still believed
that Bulger wasn't without his good points. Bulger
however still took some delight in his own devilish
naughtiness.

Not Squirt! He was tired. He understood little
but he sensed too much. People were wont to
remark, — some people will be kind — that public
demand for the *outré*, obvious, and clever, had
ruined a good man. But Squirt was too tired to
know what a state of literary ruination that
meant.

From Maine

Ronald Wallace arose every morning at nine o'clock, and putting on his lounging slippers and bath robe, lighted the gas stove, and put upon it the coffee pot, replenished with fresh coffee every other morning, rinsed out and given new coffee and fresh water three times a week. While the coffee was coming to the point of boiling he would wash his teeth and face. Of late months he sometimes forgot to wash his teeth, and recalling it later on in the day would be annoyed with himself.

If he had commissions to paint any pictures, he would set to work at ten o'clock exactly, whether he was using a model or not. If the paper house which was using a series of biblical illustrations in their advertising campaign had given him no new assignments he would sit down and read after having his coffee, with bread and fried eggs.

His studio was a big place; kept clean it would have smelled musty because the building was an old one, but draperies, costumes he'd purchased, numerous art periodicals dating back as far as twenty years, lay in heaps in corners of the room, or were stacked upon chairs, trunks or cabinets; and these added to the mustiness of the odour in his place.

For the last two years he'd stopped reading « light » novels, stories of adventure on the sea, and of romance in gay social, and bohemian art, cities in Europe. The subject of religion was bothering him, particularly because of the war and many young men who went down to death, and who, « might better never have been born for all they got out of life, if there is no after life. »

Every time a model posed for him who would talk, or be at all interested in the subject of spiritualism, Ronald would do much more resting and discussing that subject than he would do painting. « Not that I really accept it — but you can't know, you know », he would state frequently as he talked.

« My uncle in Maine — he's sixty-five years old and lives alone in a big house, with only an old woman for a housekeeper, keeps saying in his letters that I'm alone too much, and should come and stay with him. Ha, ha, that's him. Poor old soul, he's lonely, and wanting to put it off on me. I see people. Almost every week I have a model posing for me; and whenever I go out on the street to buy groceries, or to get fresh air I see people; sometimes people I know. And I like to talk to just ordinary people, clerks, the newswoman », he said to his model one day, as he was painting a picture that looked like a Sundayschool card illustration. It was to illustrate, with a series of others, the history of writing, and in it an Egyptian king was dictating to his secretary who chipped out the dictation in stone. Both the king and the secretary had on flowing garments. The same model and the same bathrobe had served for both figures. Ronald was painstaking, consulting a book he had several times to be sure that he should miss none of the details of the period which he was illustrating.

« One can't know though ; see the design on that sleeve now » he said, pointing to a picture in the book, « that's not chronological. Most illustrators are careless about such points. » But after a moment's indecision he painted in the design as it was in the book.

Ronald was the kind of man, particularly the kind of artist, about whom it is easy to remark « ineffective », and beyond which it is difficult to make remarks which distinguish him. A paunch of soft flesh had grown about his once slender body in the last five years; his stomach obtruded; his eyes were vaguely, ageing blue. Almost any bank clerk, or bookkeeper, past thirty five, and drooping into the fleshiness of drifting middle age, could have posed for a portrait of him. If the resemblance -

were not quite exact — few people knew Ronald, and fewer still noted his appearance to have remarked the inexactness.

During the course of three hours Ronald would generally have told any number of strange incidents about people he'd heard about, or knew somebody who knew ; incidents not quite explainable in a rational way.

« I don't believe in spiritualism exactly you know, but it's something to study ; it's in the air, you know. After all it's not much we understand. Now only the other morning I woke up thinking that my uncle was in trouble ; and that afternoon I got a letter saying he'd been quite ill.... That may be only a coincidence, but you can't know what is in the dust floating about you. »

Quite generally the model posing for him had stories to add to his. Life is mysterious ; others than models are ready to discuss, and question, and wonder, and wander, — perhaps — well strange things do happen — reality itself is often the most unreal of qualities.

One model however, a jaded-minded being, tired of discussion, and wanting not to be put to the effort of listening and answering said to Ronald :

« The subject does not interest me ; true or untrue all of the stories written up and in circulation, it does not interest me. There's nothing I can do about it ; perhaps I can do something about things more rational — « one world at a time » for me. »

The remark did not discourage Ronald in his conversation however; it was probably too apathetically spoken.

« But if one could speak with the dead, or in some way be in touch with them ? »

« We are in touch with the dead; dead ideas, dead traditions, dead moralities — aren't there enough people amongst the ones called alive because they breathe, to inflict their dull ideas on one. Why resuscitate the legion of harmless but oppressively stupid many dead beloved ones that have gone before us into that dim unkown ? »

The groping, hoping, sentimental naïveté of Ronald was hurt by the remark. That one time was the last time which that model, posed for him; but it did not matter. Existence went on, somehow, for them both.

Probably the dependent clutching of Ronald to spiritualism, for a fancied value it gave to his entity — one launched into eternity with other spiritualistic entities then — was a more clinging clutch as time went on.

There was in his hopefulness about the subject an indecision and incompetence; but these attitudes typified his attitudes in general. For a certain length of time, fifteen years before at the art school, Ronald had had a certain flair for the rebellious and self-identified in painting, which flair was due to friendship with men of more reckless dispositions than his own. During that period he was given to scoffing at his own New England type of training, and the narrow conceptions of morality that had been bred into him. For all his scoffing however the walls of restraint were up within him. Possibly if he had not been given a prize in school that made him hopeful that he might later secure the Prix de Rome, the stir of unrest, and discontent with life for convention, would have carried him on into further discovery; but the prize was the flattering hand that petted and cajoled him back, so that he applied himself earnestly to the study of the old masters — well to study no doubt — so that now any quality of mind or spirit that Ronald possessed was in no way unique to Ronald.

His studio was in a huge barnlike tenement on fourteenth street, in the seventh avenue direction off Greenwich Village. Outside his shuttered windows people pass, pass, pass; night long, and through the day in continual streams. Through the opened shutters the beat of feet came to him, tapping upon his consciousness at night as he lay in bed at the back end ot his room. After twelve o'clock at night the lights on the street were dimmed so that the streaks of light across the floor of his studio were faint and wavering; by two o'clock few people would pass his window any longer. When they did however he almost always heard them, as he slept lightly, verging on the conscious till well along five in the morning.

There are innumerable cats in that section of

New York; and the voice qualities are as various as their number is many. Contralto, tenor, minor-dramatic soprano.

Some nights, after reading books on spiritualism, or upon occult science, Ronald would put out the lights in his room and get into bed. Thoughts went revolving in his mind — O perhaps not thoughts — questions, reflections, doubtings, vague restless fears. Such times there was often added to his mental chaos the chaos of hungers in his body, in his blood too, for it seemed to him that a powdered drug had put a gluey taste of desire into his mouth, and an sting of desire into his limbs and blood. His whole body seemed itching as though cobwebs and dust were clinging to him. Then perhaps the cats would start their ghoulish baby-moaning yowls. In scampering about, screeching, groaning tortuously, they made thumps and bumps that startled him in his halfwaking state. On windy nights, when doors were banging back and forth, and there was a general rattle in the wind, it seemed as though he were resting on some insecure precipice that might give way, leaving him to fall — to fall — to fall — into some abysmal inferno, into regions of horrible tragic-voiced brutes of prey.

Often it would be ten minutes before he could tell himself, and believe, that the shreiking outside was only that of cats; the clatter only that of rubbish in the wind, of doors and window shutters banging. Because in his mind also were images beckoning and threatening; playing dramas that past in a moment seemed to him continuing through eternity; dramas of desire and of denial; of almost realization then collapse.

At last however the night would pass; at about five or six — as light began to come on and reality became something actual, clear enough to be seen with his own eyes, — he would go to sleep, and wake exactly, of his own accord, at nine o'clock. He was given to be rather boastful of that; that he needed no alarm clock and never, positively never overslept, whether he had work to do or only would pass the day in reading and puttering about his studio in never completed room cleanings. No one could ever accuse Ronald of not having regular habits, if that is a matter about which there shall be accusation.

When he had arisen he made his coffee; while it was coming to the point of boiling, he washed and dressed. Then — if a model came in — he would ask the model's judgment about the appearance of a hand, or a drapery, or a group arrangement in the illustration he was working upon.

Otherwise he read; generally books on spiritualism, or on the occult... One never knows.

Temperment

When Hannah Carp, eighty–six years old, brought a suit of divorce against her husband, Michael, aged ninety, charging that he had not contributed to her support for years, and that all he wanted to do was « to hang around and pester a body », the worthy gentleman took it philosophically. It wasn't probable that he would have a great deal of further use for a wife.

« Hannah always has been and always will be tempermental », he declared, and for the rest was chivalrously silent.

Whether it was the possession of temperment that had caused Hannah to lead the variegated life that she had lead, or whether it takes a person of temperment to survive through such a life is too fine a point to be decided here; as fine a point perhaps as the number of angels who could dance on the point of a pin.

When fifteen, Hannah, then Hannah Ruggles, and a buxom, swarthy skinned lass she was, with cold blue eyes and yolk yellow hair — her eyes

had fire in them for all their cold blueness —
when fifteen, she wearied of her home in the Kent-
ucky Mountains, where what labour is done is
done mainly by women. A trifle morose in those
days, not given to words, she didn't bother using
any to tell her father that she was heading for the
lowlands. Nevertheless to the lowlands she went,
and a year later could have been seen — if one
looked soon enough — working in a laundry.
However, Hannah, while not objecting to work,
did not like the monotony of laundry work. There
was a better living to be had out on the street.
Hannah had it.

Hannah also had a few month's rest in a Girls
Corrective Home; but Hannah couldn't be held in
for any two years, as her sentence dictated. The
first time she departed, she was found and returned
within the course of a month; the second time
Hannah decided that Louisville had always been
just a starting point in her career anyway.

It was not till she was almost twenty that Hannah
was sentenced to the penitentiary for being accom-
plice to a holdup man who had killed at least two
of his victims. Because the first year or so away
from home Hannah's sense of morality kept her
from pilching private property. However, upon
finding society so prone to interfere with her disposition of her own personal favours, she became
calloused, and a little embittered. Bitterness is a
pitfall.

Hannah did her ten years in the penitentiary. Upon release she was still a hardy specimen, but less apt to appeal to a street clientele than in earlier years. What can a woman do under such circumstances ? — Hannah did it. And if the house she conducted had a name for being rather rough — some people always will have too much sensibility.

Within the next twenty years Hannah served a sentence or so now and then in corrective institutions, at workhouses, and one time spent two years in a state penitentiary other than the one in which she'd spent her first sentence. Hannah always was a good spender. If she liked a person — there you were. She liked him or her and if there was anything Hannah could do for that person — presto — done. If she didn't like a person, or to put it strongly, if she disliked a person — eyes and ears are ordinary things — there was only one man who permanently lost the sight of one eye, and it never was discovered who delivered old Tim Murphy the blow that killed him.

When Hannah had arrived at the age of fifty, whatever she had in the way of a reputation, she also had quite a great deal of property : farms that she had bought herself; mining land that prospectors had diced away to her during the years she'd run a gambling house in conjunction with — other enterprises. One man had willed her all his considerable property because he had no relatives and she seemed a cheery body.

In consequence of which possessions Hannah was a widow upon whom the rough and ready specimens of California, mining men, stockmen, adventursome spirits generally, did not look with indifferent eyes. She was right comely, and peppery for a woman of her years. Men always do like spirit, whether it be in a bucking bronco or in a woman.

Why it was that Hannah married Michael Carp, than whom a meeker soul never existed, and who had no property to speak of, and wasn't a man in the sense that you'd think Hannah would understand the term, no one could understand. Nobody tried to for long because out of the scene, out of mind also, is a general rule in new country, and Hannah went, soon after marrying Michael, to live with him on a farm in a quiet farming community.

For thirty years she lived with him. She cooked their meals and kept the house in tip-top shape as such unimproved houses go. There wasn't a quieter, better behaved woman in the community than Hannah. O yes, she read Michael the riot act once in a while — but be reasonable, she was a woman, a wife, a human being. Hannah might have gone to church if someone had informed her that it was the thing to do, but the church was twelve miles from the Carp's farm, and the life of a farmer's wife is a busy life. Between getting the cows milked, butter made, eggs marketed, soil plowed, seed planted, grains harvested, hay cut and stored in the barn — in all of which activities Hannah took a hand — a woman isn't going to think about church when she's never thought about it, and doesn't quite know what it signifies.

For the last five years of the thirty however Hannah had been able to attend to few things; her mind would go back on her in giving orders to the help. So she and Michael had gotten rid of their farm and moved to town. Then Michael was about all the day long, wanting to talk, or ask questions in a quavering voice. Hannah never had been a woman of words.

So Hannah got a divorce; and Michael was very philosophical about it. There's only one thing to do when a person is tempermental, and that's to accept the fact.

The Town Builder

When Mrs. Forsyth came into the room from a drive in the country — she was the only person in town who retained a buggy and coachman — she was in a voluminous white linen gown, and was waving away the heat from her with a huge palm fan. « I am so glad to see you my boy », she said, extending her hand, her entire arm in fact, to me, from across the room, and walking with a consciously free, almost dramatic manner. She always gave the impression of being a renowned actress, or a duchess with gracious, vivacious dignity.

Of course I didn't know how much of the story she told me about having planned the town of Compton herself was true. Like self-made people generally she liked to talk about her feats, and to reminisce about her climb upwards. It was true, I'd heard from other town's-people, that thirty years before she'd run a boarding house for the men who worked at the railroad shops. It was true that she owned at least one hundred houses in town. There was no reason to disbelieve that she had supervised the erection of all of them, and had planned them too.

« This town wouldn't have so much park space, such wide streets, and numbered streets and avenues if I hadn't made a map of how it should be eventually, twenty five years back », she told me. Then she insisted that I have lemonade. « I'll help you through college too, my boy », she volunteered quite out of the clear sky. « I understand human nature ; I trust people and my trust has never been betrayed yet. »

Mrs. Kennedy, at whose house I roomed, sniffed whenever I talked about Mrs Forsyth, who, to my way of thinking was a remarkable woman. « She is if you believe her. There are others who don't talk so much about their remarkability », Mrs. Kennedy assured me. « Now, I'm not saying anything, but it looks strange to me that a woman would be able to own all the property that Mrs. Forsyth does if keeping boarders is all she got her start on. »

At other times she insinuated that hair and teeth were not the only artificial things about Mrs. Forsyth. Mrs. Kennedy was a good house-keeper, an honest woman, who dressed simply, and had no show about her. « If I was to wear perfume it wouldn't smell like cornstarch, you can know that », she said to me one night as I came up the walk to the veranda of her house, upon which veranda she sat rocking a major portion of the day, to see what she could see and to converse with whoever passed by. Only the natural subtlety

of own mind jerked it from its mood of abstraction,
and weariness with the heat to connect the comment in some way with Mrs. Forsyth.

There was no use of my saying that I didn't think
Mrs. Forsyth had a wooden leg, but simply walked
stiffly because she was well nigh sixty years old.
I'd never seen enough of Mrs. Forsyth to know
whether she had wooden leg or not.

« It's simply as a personality that Mrs. Forsyth
strikes me as unique. Of course she has distinct
limitations I suppose » — I remarked then to Mrs.
Kennedy.

« If limitations was all she had it wouldn't
matter », she said, and left me to imagine for myself
the worse things Mrs. Forsyth had.

There was no getting around the fact that Mrs.
Forsyth indulged in a lot of pilaver. Every time I
met her on a down town street she'd stop to tell
me about how some grocer tried to overcharge her,
simply because she had money ; how in spite of
the fact of owning much property she was a poor
woman. « Land poor, I am. I lie awake nights
scheming to get hold of money to meet my tax
bills. »

But she was likable — to me anyway — a breezy
old liar to be sure. A man of the world sort of an
old woman. Once in a while she would tell me
some of the stories she'd said at other times she
could tell me if I weren't so young.

I was sorry when it came towards the end of

summer that she would skoot down side streets
whenever she saw me coming. I wished she could
have understood that at least three years before
that time I'd learned not to take any stock in
exhuberant promises to « help me through college » or « start me in business ». It never would be
staid dependable qualities that would recommend
such people as Mrs. Forsyth to the world, and
I knew that.

But she never talked about her children, or even
her business for long. Amongst the grocery-minded
populace of Compton her quality was unique, and
not cramped with prayer-meeting attitudes. There
was more truth in her lies than in the austerest
truthfulness of anybody else I knew there. Dear
old lady. She's probably dead now. And if she is,
she's liver that anybody who's living in Compton
at the present moment. She surely left land for a
park to be named after her, or provisions in her
will to build a public building that should comme-
morate her.

The Psychoanalyzed Girl

Dania wasn't in the room five minutes before she was telling whoever it was that sat near her that « I am all tangled up psychologically. I have the mother, and brother complex. »

She was a strange girl, Dania, that is to a person not used to strange girls, and people who live in « Bohemian quarters ». In Paris she could be seen walking about the Montparnasse district with a Paisley shawl thrown over her shoulders, a many-colored beribboned hat, mauve stockings, or pale green — some exotic colour always — and the skirt that showed beneath her coat made of Paisley shawl was generally a corded silk one with red, white, and green, broad and thread, stripes.

Needless to say people noticed her as she went by. They might have noticed her anyway, had she dressed quietly, because her eyes were soft brown, shaded with impossibly long eyelashes; her skin was bronze olive, and days when it might look sallow, Dania knew just how much rouge to put on to give her cheeks a warm glowing appearance.

Very narrow shoulder she had drawn up within
herself usually. She contradicted her own manner,
giving alternately a quiet, mouselike impression, a
hard embitteredly sophisticated one, and again an
impression of confused, wounded naive child-
ishness.

« I don't know how to be happy, that's me; don't
know to have a good time, and when all these
Americans here want me to go around I can't find
any pleasure in the noisy things they do », she
said, one day as I walked down the Boulevard
Raspail with her. « There ! that's me. Analyzing
myself again. Why can't I leave myself alone ? »

« You are suffering from life rather than from
sickness, Dania », I commented. « Don't look so hard
for happiness, and stay away from the Bohemians
at the Rotonde who are neither labourers, artists,
nor intelligent — only moping incompetents, sca-
vangers of the art world. »

One day Dania hailed me from across the street,
so we joined each other and went walking down
the street together. It wasn't till afterwards that I
remembered how artfully Dania managed to stop
and ask a direction of a young Frenchman, who
was a helper about a piano van-wagon.

After talking about where a certain street was
for five minutes, very conscious that his eyes were
admiring her with open curiosity and desire in
them she came on saying : « Ain't he the handsome
devil though. »

« There you are, Dania ; you say you want experience. He'll take you on. Look back. His eyes are following you yet. »

The young Frenchman was a swarthy, black-eyed being ; with lithe energy. He was wearing a red shirt, and had a red scarf bound about his waist making a corsage for him. Except for Dania he'd simply have been part of the local colour of the quarter for me. Now I wondered whether he was from the South of France, or of Spanish or Italian descent. There'd been boldness, respect too, in his attitude towards Dania. He must have been Paris bred not to have had some shyness in him.

Another day I ran into Dania, and we passed the young Frenchman again, loading furniture into a van. He looked at Dania, and an expectant look came into his eyes. Dania was returning his glance from under her long eyelashes, and flick-ered a tiny smile at him, whereupon his entire set of straight teeth showed in a smile.

« He always smiles at me now », Dania said.

« You pass him often do you ? »

« O yes, I usually manage to come down this street at about the same time everyday, when he's coming in on the van to the storage house to put up the truck... Isn't it ridiculous though. He catches my fancy, but of course I couldn't. »

« Rats, Dania, take a chance. Start something with him, if he doesn't with you ; and he will if you'll bat your eye the right way. Why stand on the threshold of « experience » eternally saying that you don't live, but merely exist. You must set Rome afire if you're going to sit watching the flames with enjoyment. »

It was useless for me to remark however. The last time I saw Dania, two months after that day, she said « I'll have to go back to New-York and get psychoanalized. I must find out why I can't have average emotions, and enjoy life just a little bit. »

« Tut, tut, woman. Some of them there will be telling you again that you're setting out to hurt yourself because of perverse instinct in you when you slip on a wet floor because of new shoes. »

If one could be sure that Dania enjoyed her unhappiness as the only thing she dared permit to give importance to her egotium... But there she is — in Paris — Dania.

The Fast Girl

Jerry Jenkins was not at all like his brother, Deacon Samuel Jenkins; he was a « rake » a « roue » a « cheap sport » who would stand on the pool hall corner and make comments about women's ankles as they went by. My sisters always became frigid with hauteur when passing him. But, not to let my sisters know about it, I found him much more tolerable than the Deacon. He slipped me a nickel about every time he saw me; the Deacon always looked at me as though his austere sense of the righteous was shocked.

Jerry wore patent leather shoes, and a sporty vest; his keen brown eyes didn't miss much attractive in the way of woman–flesh that struck town; but his sharp featured brown face didn't have so ferret–like a look as the Deacon's. He at least was liberal with his money, and it was he who'd given Sue Gallagher money enough to get out of town when she was going to have a baby, which he was not responsible for either.

Yet every respectable woman in town disapprov-
ed of him; and the men in town, even if they
didn't dislike him, had enough things to explain
to their wives generally without getting the name
of being the same kind of man that Jerry was by
being seen with him. No one could blame Mrs. Jenkins for having divorced him ; maybe no one
could blame Jerry for having let her, after seeing
the lady, but when a man and wife are the parents
of two nearly grown children it's supposed that a
man's old enough to settle down.

Louise Dutton was a striking looking girl. The
fellows in town, also the ladies, were divided into
two parties regarding their opinions about her.
One party said that Louise rouged, screwed like
a mink, and only got away with it because she
was clever; the other side said that her colour was
naturally vivid, and that simply because her
mother was poor and had to take in sewing, people
gossiped about Louise, who wasn't nearly as careless in her manners and actions as other girls
whose families were well fixed.

The first time Jerry noticed her and said « Who's
that pippin » and was told, he added « For Christ's
sake, it doesn't seem yesterday that she was
tearing around town in knee dresses, and with a
running nose. She's learned how to keep her face
clean and dress like a million dollar race horse
hasn't she ? »

What happened to Louise would not have

occurred had it not been for Jake Murray and Dave Thomson. They worked at the roundhouse and were a wild sort of lowbrow. After coming back from the city, where he'd had a job as travelling salesman for a men's notion house, Dave'd taken to being flashier than ever. Jake was another of the same kind except that he'd get converted about every three years when an evangelist came to town, and instead of strutting around town showing of his bullying strength he'd take on the job of Sunday School superintendent for a time — till his backsliding. He'd be given the job in the hope that responsibility would bolster him up.

It was on halo'een night when gangs of boys, youths, and men — one man as old as fifty, and several well towards thirty — had collected all over town. At about ten thirty the gangs had all marched down a back street of town and there were so many marching that the procession was four blocks long, marching in such a straggling manner as they did. The special policemen in town couldn't do much. The various gangs turned over outhouses, dumped hayracks into the town pond, poured tar on the main highschool building steps; stole bell clappers, and piled privies, wagons, and barrels of ashes before schoolhouse doors, churches, and county buildings.

It was one o'clock and most of the boys and youths had gone home. At any rate the various gangs had separated, but Jake Murray, Dave

Thomson, and about eighteen men were standing around planning some new devilment to get into. Several of the men were nearly drunk. All were noisy, profane, and « to hell with everything » in their attitudes.

Louise Dutton had been dancing at the town dance hall until twelve, and had stayed talking to various fellows and girls who'd come into the ice-cream parlor that she'd stopped at to drink soda water on her way home. Just as she was turning the corner leading from Main street to her home, an avenue that ran past the town theatre, some of the men in Jake's gang recognized her. It didn't take more than a remark or so, and a suggestion, for them to decide to hold her and make her talk to them.

It was Jake who grasped her wrist as she came along and chucked her under the chin.

« You cowardly brute », she said, and tried to jerk away. That angered him, and he grabbed her to him and placed his face so near to her that she could feel his breath.

« Don't you kiss me, you animal », she exclaimed.

« O it ain't kissing I'll do to you », he said. « What about it fellows. She's too good with her airs, and we all know what she is. Let's have a good time. »

It did Louise no good to protest, or to appeal to the group in the hope that someone would protect her. There were some harmless enough fellows in the crowd; Dutch Simmons, who drove a grocery delivery wagon ; Bill Peters, a haberdashery clerk in the town's one mens furnishing store. But these harmless fellows didn't have the guts to go up against Jake Murray and Dave Thomson.

No one knows whether all the men in the crowd actually did « have a good time » with Louise or not, but she had to be carried home. Some of the fellows carried her, saying that if she was found laying out on the street by the policeman there'd be an investigation and trouble for them all.

There was no investigation. Louise was sick for several days. When finally she came out again and was seen on the street many girls refused to speak to her. Men, particularly the men who'd been in that gang, treated her with familiar contempt. One day as she was going by Jake Murray he made some slurring remark to her. She turned a blazing gaze on him, lifted her head, and walked on.

She did not appear often on the streets any more, and when she did she would not look at anybody, or speak to anybody, but walked erect looking through all people. So many people she knew had cut her that she burned with anger at everybody. One day she was going by the pool hall corner, towards the post office however, when she heard a voice :

« Miss Dutton. »

She turned and saw that it was Jerry Jenkins speaking to her. Her first impulse was to jerk her head up and walk on, but she concluded that now her reputation was such that to talk to him could not make it worse. Furthermore his tone, at least, was respectful. So she stopped, saying « Yes ? »

« I guess you'd like to be able to get out of town and never see this place again wouldn't you ? » Jerry asked her.

« Like to, yes — that takes money. I will get out of town soon, but can't right now », she answered.

« Let me help you. I'm going to Minneapolis myself in a few days », he hesitated, watching her face, which expressed little of what she might be feeling. After a moment he went on. « Of course it wouldn't be a good idea for us to leave town together, but — you could meet me in Minneapolis. »

« Yes, I could », she emphasized the *could* a trifle. « Yes », she smiled, « if you want to arrange that, I am willing. »

Jerry walked down towards the post-office with her, and while doing so, took his wallet out of his pocket, and extracted ten twenty dollar bills, which he gave to her, under cover of his hand, being careful that no one should see him.

« I'll be at the Hôtel H..... in Minneapolis next Monday. You can register there under the name of Mrs. Jenkins if you wish », he told Louise.

She took the money and soon after left Jerry.

Two weeks later Jerry came back to town after a trip to Minneapolis. He had not seen Louise Dutton. She had left the home town ten days before. Neither Jerry, nor the town ever saw her again.

Sometime later Jerry commented on the fact that he'd made an arrangement with Louise to meet him in Minneapolis.

« I'm for that girl; damned sorry I didn't give her a thousand dollars while I was at it; if I'd known she wouldn't show up I would have. »

People joshed Jerry about the trick Louise had played on him for several years. « The old rake, that's the time he got fooled », they would say.

A Business Family

Business 'had been rather good at the *Rest an:
Hour* Kosher yearround hotel, because it was an
easy place to get to from New–York City on only a
weekend holiday. Mrs. Sturgeon, the married
daughter of Ike Rosenstein, who owned the place
but who had too many romantic ideas about the
necessity of going to added expense to serve his
guests real kosher food, was quite cross. Between
argueing with her parents, running to her two year
old baby when she cried — which was often for the
infant was petulant and viciously yelpy — it was all
Mrs. Sturgeon could do to go with proper dignity
about her duties. She was builded somewhat on the
lines of a pouter pidgeon to aid her through.

« A resort like this is no place for an invalid.
I wish Mr. Davis would take his wife away; it's all
right through the middle of the week to have her
here, but we can't pay her all the attention she
requires over the weekend rush », Mrs. Sturgeon
stated several times to the hotel clerk.

Mrs. Davis was a sick woman. Some guests at the

hotel declared that she put on. At the approach of
a newcomer, it is true, she, usually relapsing in an
arm chair, would ooze further into it, seeking to
resemble a jellyfish in helpless flabbiness as she ran
over the arms of the rocker. Such times as she arose
to walk, to go to meals, or to be helped to her room,
she poured and rippled over the floor, slowly, and
without undue rhythm. At intervals she would stop
and place a doughlike hand to her forehead to
indicate great pain and strain there — that was not
mental. Mrs. Davis looked extremely feeble. Given
a word, and she would flow with conversation about
her aliments to anybody but her children, Fania,
and Randolph, both of whom treated her with
insolent indifference except when utilizing her
powers over « the old man » to obtain capital for
them.

The hotel clerk upon going out to the kitchen
after hours sometimes — tiptoeing, and observing
cautiously that none of the bosses were around —
found Mrs. Davis there. She would smile at him
half shame facedly and apologize : « I can't eat my
meals so I have to have bread and butter between
times », whereupon he'd scout around and get sweet
butter for her because she'd confided to him that
she didn't dare for she'd drop dead sure if Mrs.
Sturgeon saw her swiping butter.

One Friday night, « Fania » Davis, named by her
parents « Fannie », was at the resort hotel trying
to bid up the price which her father would give her

upon marriage from one thousand to thirty thousand dollars. Her affianced one sat at the dinner
table with Fania, and her father and mother, and
he was not silent on the subject either, because the
fact that he was also Fania's cousin added
familiarity to his flip Semitic assurances that the
money'd stay in the family anyway.

The young man's face was wax-shiny; his eyes
were glistening; his lips were sensuous red globules.
There was passionate impetuousness in his manner
of assuring his Uncle that the investment would
be as good business as any shipment of bootleg
whiskey that every netted Mr. Davis fifty thousand
dollars in two weeks time.

« A physician can't get the swell people patronizing him without enough money to have real
classy furnishing in his office; a big suite of rooms,
upholstered furniture, and oriental rugs. I'm just
marrying Fania because she's my cousin and her
money might as well stay in the family. But I'll
have to marry Rosie Baumberger if you can't start
me off right », Michael asserted, whereupon Fania
wept, and when her father remained adamant,
assuring the « childer » that, knowing how they
spent money, he'd rather give it to them as they
needed it, Fania went out of the dining room in a
great tantrum, and left the hotel, saying that she
and Michael would spend the weekend elsewhere.
In the background of her mind was the knowledge,
that should she remain away long enough her

mother would worry, and that would make her mother ill, and then to get Fania to come to her mother, Papa Davis would have to acquiesce to Fania's demands. There was no sentimentality in either Fania or Michael.

Soon after Fania and Michael had departed, Randolph Davis came in, late for dinner as usual, and said he couldn't wait to eat, but would take the car and drive to New-York that night. Father Davis believed that Randolph had too good a business head, and mother Davis was too cowed by her children, for either of them to ask him his mission.

The two elderly people discussed affairs, not with reason, because Mrs. Davis refused to reason beyond the fact that Fania was her dear daughter and that Papa Harris had a million dollars anyway so that he should immediately send for Fania and assure her that she'd have fifty thousand dollars for a settlement. It is quite probable he'd have acquiesced, but soon after she'd finished eating Mrs. Davis became very ill, and called persistently for Fania and Randolph, whom she declared had deserted her forever. When a doctor arrived he said with some nonchalance — he was a village doctor, calloused to sickness, births, death, late hour calls, and hysterics — that she might, or she might not, pull through. He advised that Fania and Randolph be sent for.

It was not known however where either of them

were to reach either by 'phone or by telegram.

Sunday morning after many doctor calls, and much fuss nursing on the part of other hotel lady guests, women who sought means of passing time away with some elements of emotion in the method, Mrs. Davis died, as a new and reputedly competent doctor, called in for consultation, was examining her.

The news was broken to Mrs. Sturgeon by Mr. Davis who stumbled out upon the veranda of the hotel sobbing: « She is dead, she is dead » in great gutteral heaves of breath. Between outbursts he gave the hotel clerk thirty cents and instructions to call certain relatives informing them of the death. Habit was so strong upon him that when the operator did not get the numbers at once he would say :

« She doan'd get it. Ged the money back then. »

One lady, who had given the hotel clerk a first impression of looking like a Madonna in a simple black gown, and a later, more lasting impression of calamity personified, gained momentary attention by fainting. The clerk happened to be standing somewhat near her at the time, so was the first to pick her from the floor. It was the clerk also who received most of the vinegar splashed towards her forehead to revive her; and the clerk to whom she clung upon revival. « You don't know what a death means to us jews », she said to him then, smiling bravely, wanly, through the intensely tragic atmosphere she had summoned about her.

« My dear friend, my dear friend, Mrs. Davis — she — is — dead », the lady sobbed, recalling no doubt that she had once spent a half hour talking to Mrs. Davis as they both rocked chairs on the hotel veranda and sipped tea with sliced lemon, from a glass.

In consequence of this intimacy she was so broken up that it was quite impossible for her to recover after fainting; she could not stay another day at the hotel. Within an hour she had checked out. The clerk noticed that after paying her bill she had but five dollars left in her pocket book and wondered if that had anything to do with her not being able to stay another day, or the planned week longer, at the hotel. He did not argue with her when she declared that she owed ten dollars less than the books indicated, but accepted her figures.

Mrs. Sturgeon came in soon after the lady had paid her bill and commented upon the misfortune of Mrs. Davis' death, but admitted a little later that it was going to be bad for the hotel business this week.

« It doesn't do a place any good to have a person die in it. We ought to have insisted upon her being taken to a sanatorium. »

Soon she discovered the shortage in the lady's hotel bill payment, and would not listen to the clerk's statement that the firm had no proof that

Papa Rosenstein hadn't quoted her cheaper rates than were customary, as he was always doing. He was spared further argument for the moment however by the arrival of an undertaker's wagon, into the depths of which Mrs. Davis' remains were taken. All was silence on the veranda of the hotel except the tramping of the feet of men who carried her body, the sneezing of the undertaker's horses, the rasping breathing of an elderly lady guest, Standing at a respectful distance the hotel help, the guests, and family connections — children, nieces, brothers, — of the Rosenstein family, looked on, grave eyed.

Mr. Davis came up to the hotel clerk and whispered that he too would have to check out of the hotel now; a taxi waited to take him away.

« But you do someding for me boy. Domorrow some men calls me up on the 'phone about some liquor ve vant to get rid of. You dell' em to sell, qvick. You dell' em so, und ven I come again I pay you. Fifteen thousand dollars ve will make. » Mr. Davis whispered to the hotel clerk, with a look of triumph, and a knowing wink of his left eye. As he turned to go out of the door memory assailed him, so that upon reaching the door, he plumped against it, and stumbled out unto the veranda with a deep groan, more reflective and final than the earlier ones had been. « She is dead. She is dead », he said, with his head bent forward and trembling back and forth.

He was not seen again for two weeks at the hotel.

Then he appeared again, and informed whoever seemed interested that his daughter Fania was married, and that upon her marriage he had given « the childer » fifty thousand dollars as a present. « Dwendy thousand dollar more than they thought they'd ged. » Such was his memorial to his departed wife.

He would go out in the vacant six acre stretch of grassy land that stood before the hotel, to stand straddled legged near a lone tree at the nearest end; something in his squatting, coatless, suspendered figure gave the impression of stolid nobility — too conscious of itself in a way — and something of pathos and abstraction, a weariness that seemed to indicate a consciousness of the vainglory in human achievement clung to him. There was a sadness and gentleness about his manners.

The hotel clerk, noting his posture of solitude one day — the day of his own discharge — contemplated him for a time, wondering : Is it not such as he who are the foundations of the structure of society ?

Abrupt Decision

Mrs. Stoddard was the most charming woman in town, not beautiful or slender, not intellectual, but with a simple drawling charm about her, which, with her knowledge of how things are done in the city, — teas served with sandwiches of the right thickness, or with the Russian sized teacups and sliced lemon rather than milk — caused her to be quite admired. She evaded plumpness, and looked gently matronly. Any number of women declared that her last biscuit-brown suit was too dainty for words, and set off her soft brown hair and eyes wonderfully.

In fact the family life of the Stoddards was just what family life should be, because she governed where a woman is meant to govern, and acquiesced tactfully to her husband and two sons, only to have them yield to her in most things in the end.

Eric, the older boy, was a trifle wild, playing pool too much at the corner pool parlor, gambling some, and perhaps seen over often with girls of questionable character, but Mrs. Stoddard did not

make the error of driving him to further recklessness with nagging.

Any woman who could select a cut of steak as
Mrs. Stoddard did, exactly one inch thick, properly
tender, and cooked just beyond the point of displeasing rarity, would certainly retain her husband's
affections. After dinner at night she could still
come and sit on the arm of Frank's lounge chair,
and stroke his hair, and babble love–talk to him,
without a sign from him that he'd rather be reading his paper.

Neither of the Stoddard boys, Eric or Allen,
were exceptionally bright, but they were well–
bred, and trained to be considerate of their mother,
which in the end means more than precocity such
as Buddy Fisher's. The fact that Buddy had taken
prizes at school for an essay on Lowell as a poet;
or had at thirteen written a theme on « As you
Like It » and won honours over highschool students
six years older than he signified little actually.
Many people suspected he'd copied that theme
from somewhere anyway. It was altogether too
sophisticated sounding for a boy. Perhaps one of
his older sisters had written it. Buddy was too
nervy and fresh. Allan's quieter, shyer manner was
more attractive in a boy of that age.

Walter Simmons, however, treated Allen like a
kid, but Buddie he'd talk to much as he would to
any eighteen year old fellow he knew. Buddie
didn't hear this, and wouldn't have understood it

if he had, but Mr. Stoddard hinted once or twice to Attorney Granger that Walter's friendship for Buddie might have disagreeable connotations, since Walter was the sort of young man who didn't care for football, or any rough games, and spent too much time in the house playing Chopin and Schumann on the piano.

Buddie liked music however, liked to read, and talk about things which had happened to him that Allen didn't know anything about yet. Buddie and Walter agreed that Allen was a nice kid, and pretty game for a youngster who'd been tied to his mother's apron strings all his life. But he was so naive. Making remarks of surprise about things everybody knew and accepted. Actually he didn't know that pickles were made out of cucumbers but thought they grew on a tree like olives. Strange little lapses of intelligence there were in Allen, as though he were possessed of inability to observe the actualities about him, or to note the significence of a remark.

« I gave Allen « What Every Boy Should know » to read the other day because he was asking so many questions », Walter told Buddie once.

Buddie chuckled :

« O that's it. He's been experimenting with something I guess. That was why he was so scared this morning, wondering if all the things the book said about the dangers in jacking–off were true. »

« I didn't gather that. It must be so though. Now

that you mention it I remember he seemed worried when I was jollying him. »

Hilda, the Simmon's hired girl came out while Walter and Buddie were talking. « Hey, Hilda, we're talking about an awfly interesting subject Don't you want to join us ? » Walter asked her.

« Huh, I know what it is. Now see here don't youse boys talk vulgar to me, God damn it, I'm a lady », she answered, and they all laughed. Hilda was such a clown, and very amusing with her coarseness, though if Mrs. Simmons had kept her ears open to know what kind of girl Hilda was she would have discharged her very quickly, not because Mrs. Simmons didn't have a robust sense of humour herself, to like a good story and a hearty laugh, but a woman doesn't want a hired girl who talks too openly to her sons.

« What doings have you been up to since last night Hilda? Now, now, don't blarney me, I'll bet you let Bill O'Brien put the blocks to you. You know you can't resist the son of a banker who has as much money as his father has », Walter teased.

« I didn't; I can tell you I didn't I, wouldn't let that fellow touch me with a ten foot pole. I never let him put his hand above my knee », Hilda assured him.

« That's nearer than a ten foot pole I'd say », Buddie assured her.

« Well, I'm not so careful as I might be, but... »

« Now Hilda, you remember you said the other day you'd let one fellow have two inches before you decided you wouldn't. And it's likely you'd stop then. Tra, la, now don't expect me to believe every little story you tell me of that kind. »

Hilda turned on her heels and filled the pail which she was carrying with water from the faucet on the side of the house.

« All right sonny. But what's it to you ? What's it to you I ask. I don't let you sleep with me anyway do I ? »

Allan had come across the lawn in time to hear the last few remarks, and stood with an expression of wonder on his face. « Gosh, she doesn't care what she says or how she says it, does she », he put in after Hilda had went back into the kitchen.

Two days later Mrs. Simmons discharged Hilda, and Walter wormed it out of Allen that he'd told his mother about the conversation he'd heard. Of course Mrs. Stoddard had repeated it to Mrs. Simmons. Walter didn't care that Hilda was discharged but « you mustn't tell everything you know to your mother », he advised Allen on general principles.

Walter was one of the few people who didn't care much for Mrs. Stoddard, and thought she was too nice and correct, wanting to make her boys « perfect gentlemen » which is stupid if that's all they'd manage to be. « Hell, what's life for anyway if we can't get a little satisfaction out of it our-

selves ? » he'd say to Buddie, and then continue
talking, condemming most of the standards by
which people Buddie knew judged life. Buddie
was appaled sometimes though he wouldn't let
Walter know it.

« Appearance, that's all people care about. Look
at Mrs. Stoddard. You needn't think she doesn't
know her husband is having an affair with Kate
Langson, and that all that « lovely home life »
stuff around their house isn't show. She hasn't
the ginger to tell old Frank where to head in at,
like my mother would dad if he got gay. She sighs
around, thinking she can get him back with nice
treatment, though why any woman wants a barrel
front like him back I don't get. He's a rotter anyway ; dad says you always have to watch him in
every business deal, and only keeps up a front of
friendliness to him because he's sorry for Mrs. Stoddard. » Walter told Buddie.

After that when Buddie was at the Stoddard's,
staying for dinner with Allan, or playing checkers
in the library, he would watch Mr. and Mrs. Stoddard, and saw that many nights Mr. Stoddard failed
to come home for his meals. He was very sorry for
her, and contemptuous now of her husband.

« That guy is a damned hog beneath his smooth
manners, coming home and hinting to Mrs. Stoddard that there's nothing in her to appeal to a
man. And he used to be a bootblack. He acts like
one yet, even if he has money », Buddie would say

now, though once he'd quite envied Allen his father who'd give him so much spending money.

Evenings, when alone, Mrs. Stoddard would sit in the library with a sewing basket on her lap, and perhaps darn socks for a time, but she'd stop finally and simply sit.

Memories came drifting to her. She recollected the first time she'd met Frank when she was only seventeen, and thought him so handsome, and winning. How beautiful his head had seemed to her then with its wavey light brown hair, and the cold blue eyes that glistened when he was talking to her. She saw the Frank of then, clean-necked, tall, straight-bodied. It did not please her to put that Frank beside the present one, whose back neck had rolls of flesh upon it, and whose stomach protruded massively. Years before he had liked to hear — or declared that he did — her read poetry aloud to him, to sit and dream gently over the lines as she herself did then, and feel their love passages sublimated in his own heart — so she had thought. Not out of any reckless impulse of her own, but because of his aggressive persuasion she had eloped with him.

And housework had kept her occupied so that she was not discontented. Eric had come, and not many years later, Allen. Now after nineteen years she was for the first time reflecting what this man, her husband, actually meant to her, since he was being gradually taken away from her.

It did not astonish her to find that she felt not a
pang, except a vague fear that grew as she contemplated the situation that should a complete rift
come, she could not know what to do with herself,
not having somebody to keep a house in order,
to maintain a home and a place to entertain in for
so as to keep up social appearance necessary to
a man of financial standing. Eric would be going
to college; Allen would occupy little of her time
— time appaled her. She had not read for years;
she did not care herself for the social passtimes of
calling on ladies, giving teas, and in Minneapolis,
the city in which she had lived until her marriage,
what was there for her to do, what people to know,
should she leave Frank now?

One night as she was in the library she took out
a book of poems, that was in the case because a
well furnished home must have a library, and taste
demanded certain well known literary works. The
book opened in her hand and she read. The poem
was Shelleys's « The Moon ». Her eyes followed the
sentences, her mind understood the images, and at
the end :

« And ever changing, like a joyless eye
That finds no object for its constancy? »

made her reflect a moment. « An object worth it's
constancy. » Could she feel that he was that to her,
or was she simply his wife, and the mother of his

children because there was no other objective
which she felt more keenly desirable ?

A phrase that her mother had used to her years
before in advising her not marry Frank came into
her mind. « He is crass, and without an element of
inner refinement », and she also recalled that she
had not felt that her mother had uttered an untruth
at that time. She had responded to young energy,
and exhuberance, and asked nothing further of
him, simply because he had not opposed her finer
impulses. His « woman » to him. Now he was turning to a younger « woman ».

It was recalled to her mind at the moment, that
after having told Frank about Hilda's conversation with the boys, Frank's eyes had followed the
girl's movements with an interest that had not been
in them before, as she had been working in the
summer kitchen of the Simmons across the lawn
the last night before her discharge.

There was no contempt in her for Frank, no
condemnation. There was no contempt or condemnation in her for girls such as Hilda. What
impulse had moved her, she wondered, to tell
Mrs. Simmons about the kind of girl Hilda was.
Only a weariness possessed her, but without resignation in it and without rebellion that was not
vague and uneasy.

Allen came in and was passing up stairs to his
room, and she called to him. « Come in and kiss
me goodnight dear. Have you been enjoying your

games this evening.» Her tone had the charming
drawl customary to it as she spoke; her manner
the slow languid sweetness.

« I don't think I like Walter Simmons any more,
mother », Allen remarked, after he had kissed
Mrs. Stoddard. « He tells so many nasty stories. »

« O, you mutsn't ask too much of people, Allan.
Walter has many nice things about him and it
doesn't do to expect everything and everybody to be
quite beautiful and lovable all the time. »

Two hours later, at twelve o'clock, when Mr.
Stoddard came in, Mrs. Stoddard was still up.
Frank gave a gesture of annoyance, and a growl.

« Waiting up for me again. Can't I make you
understand that it isn't necessary ? »

« I don't know that I was waiting for you Frank.
I was trying to read some poetry that I haven't
read for years, and thinking about — many different
things...

And after a pause : « Our marriage hasn't been
a particularly satisfactory one, after all, has it
Frank! Yes, yes, perhaps it has, as marriages go.
We have never wrangled, but — »

« Nonsense. What puts that into your head.
Haven't I always given you what you wanted ? »

« Um — uh », Mrs. Stoddard sighed, and breathed
a deep breath of tired emotion. « Yes, I suppose you
have, but what about you. You find it necessary to
go to — other ladies, I shan't mention a name —

for something I fail to give you... Don't, don't flush,
I'm not censoring you. The fact that you do go
elsewhere means that you want to, and if you
want to...

« O Frank, I am quite, quite tired. Let's not talk
about this matter. I'm sorry I mentioned it. I think
I'll go to bed now.» And she rose, leaned over
Frank's chair to kiss him on the forehead, and
went out into the hallway and up the stairs.
Frank watched her going, with a fury of impotent
resentment in his heart.

« One does tire of silent and weary superiority »,
he spoke as she reached the stairway.

« Why Frank, you don't think I feel — » she
began, but did not finish her sentence. Maybe he
was right. At the head of the stairway she turned
so that she could see the back of his head showing
over the top of his arm chair, enough so that she
could see the beginning fleshiness where head united
with neck. An overpowering wave of surprise
swept over her, that she had ever, that she now,
lived with that man. If his body had ever attracted her, it could not now, and could not have
for years, and there was in him no mind, no kindliness — no lack of kindliness — nothing that
signified to her. Little wonder that they had never
wrangled. He liked an easy relationship, and was
so utterly foreign in his elements to hers, that
there was no basis for wrangling. Still she could
not feel that she had claims to a feeling of super-

iority, since she had done nothing to mark her a superior being.

The next morning Mrs. Stoddard looked across the length of the breakfast table wincing with reflection, watching Frank as he sipped his coffee and was not aware that she was looking into him. At last she spoke :

« I don't think your remark last night was quite fair to me, Frank. I haven't ever felt superior to you ; I don't believe I have ever thought how I felt. Life just went on and I let it... » her speach dribbled into the silence indecisively. Frank almost ignored the remark. Then she went on :

« You don't care though, I understand now, what l have or have not felt. Neither do I care. We are each too mediocre to continually attract the other. It has taken just this little break in our relationship to make me understand how dull I am, and you are. That realization the fancied business of household duties has kept me from till now. »

« Why talk about it then. What do you want ? Whatcha driving at ? » Frank growled out.

Mrs. Stoddard was too aware of the street boy tang that still lingered in Frank's speach. She remained silent, and soon he departed for his office. Allen and Eric came down to breakfast soon, both a bit sullen, and this morning no gracious realization that morning is a heavy time of day came to aid Mrs. Stoddard to talk cheerily to them.

« Did you hear about Gay⁹ Allen », Eric said, after he had crunched away on toast for a time. « She's eloped with that butcher clerk of Garison's. Had to, I'll bet. I thought she was getting rather casual. »

« Well, don't be hard on her if she did have to, Eric. You know yourself that townlife here isn't calculated to please à high-spirited young person, boy or girl », Mrs. Stoddard advised.

It was Saturday. After breakfast Mrs. Stoddard had Allen hitch up the pony to take her out to the dairy farm on the outskirts of town and get sweet butter which was made especially for her. As the two jogged alone the country road, the tranquillity of the scene struck Mrs. Stoddard's senses unpleasantly. Not that the air wasn't clear, and an odour of alfalfa hay in the breeze as usual ; not that gophers were less alert, or the cud-chewing cattle in pastures along the way less placid. Possibly it was the placidity that was a dull wave smothering her.

Surely, like a tuberculin germ, a consciousness of the ravaging mediocrity of her existence, of days going in drab routine towards no end to which her expectancies arose, was eating into her. An impulse of affection which caused her to cuddle Allen in her arms and kiss him, passed finally, and she was contemplating and analyzing the possibilities of his future, and finding little to make her believe it would be a great one.

« Did you know that, Hilda is staying with Mrs.
Aikens. » Allen asked her after they had driven
along in silence for some time. Mrs. Aikens was
reputed to be maintaining a house of ill fame and
Allen's boy's curiosity regarding such places was
awakening.

« She might better be with Mrs. Simmons hadn't
she ? » Mrs. Stoddard said. « I rather regret having
told Mrs. Simmons of how Hilda talked to you
boys. She is young. A few years in a respectable
family and she'd probably have settled down
more. » She did not add, though she thought « but
what does it matter, one way or the other ? » She
could not let Allen know how complete a sense of
the futility of all thing possessed her.

At the dairy farm, while they waited for the
maid to put their sweet butter into a receptacle
for them to carry it away in, Mrs. Stoddard talked
to Mrs. Rankin, the wife of the farm owner.

« I feel sometimes as though my work were
never ended », Mrs Rankin was saying. « And it
becomes rather embarrassing for me too, when
Mr. Rankin and all the men are far out in the field
working, and only the maid and I are here. So
many people from town have the habit now of
bringing their milk cows out to be... » she hesitated, and looked significently at Allen, who was
hearing alertly beneath a manner of abstracted
indifference which he had suddenly assumed.

« Yes, yes. I can understand », Mrs. Stoddard

said. Then quickly, as if a sudden gasp of breath had hurt her : « O is there nothing but that — that — is that the sole motive of life ? I've been trying to remember the last day or so what I used to want of life, to make my romances of. Surely not this round of eating, sleeping, and — that. »

For the first time in years a searing flame was in her heart, a protest against life, a protest that swelled up within her and raged helplessly. She thought of escape, realizing that she was always to be with herself so that there was no escape; alwaysbe with people so that there was no escape; and this afternoon she was giving a tea to several ladies. Mrs. Fitzgerald would come in and talk about the scandalous way Mrs. Harmon's daughter acted, till Mrs. Harmon came in, and then the two of them would spar back and forth about catholics and protestants. The same people would be spoken of and criticized; the bringing up of the same children would be mooned over.

The tea was of course just as she had anticipated. There were remarks made about this girl having « had to marry » or about that lady who'd had a baby « none too long after her marriage ». Mrs. Fitzgerald had the new news to report that Mrs. Williams had told her that her grocer said he suspected Mrs. Frayne was a kleptomaniac.

« And you should have hear the remark Carrie Andrews — she is such a sharp, witty little girl — made to my daughter Loraine. She'd heard that

Nellie Frayne wanted a wristwatch, and so she said: « just tell her to let her mother know about it, and with her ability as a kleptomaniac the trick's done. » My I had to laugh at that, though I suppose one should pity the poor creature. »

After tea Mrs. Stoddard went up to her room. She did not appear at the dinner table that night at the usual time. After a time her husband, rather crossly, sent Allen upstairs to see the reason. In a minute or so he heard a terrified exclamation, and rushed upstairs. Very shortly he was at the telephone, trembling, perspiring all over his body, and particulary noticeably on his face. Within fifteen minutes both a doctor and a coroner had arrived.

« Yes, yes, I've noticed — I've noticed — that — my wife — a — Mrs. Stoddard has been acting rather strangely — her mind must have been affected — she couldn't have otherwise — not that way — with a razor. »

Mrs. Stoddard had left no note. A certain expectancy regarding life that such an action would have required had not possessed her at the moment when, after handling the instrument of her death she had almost involuntarily and unthinkingly, out of pure apathetic despair, done violence to herself.

Less than a year after this, Mrs. Fitzgerald, Mrs. Harmon, and many other ladies found ample material for tea conversation in the fact that Mr. Stoddard was married again, and had gone with his new wife to live in Minneapolis. They were all shocked; and amazed that neither Allen nor Eric Stoddard showed any signs of grief whatever.

But neither Frank, nor the mentioned ladies, nor any of the other beings who had walled in Mrs. Stoddard's life, could believe that she was anything but insane to have left them all with so little warning.

A Vacation's Job

« A Telegram », his mother said as soon as Dave came in for breakfast. « It came last night but you will stay out till all hours come what may. »

He opened it with nonchalance, feverish internally only. « Come at once; flood expected », it read and was signed by his engineer friend, Paul Somerland.

« I'll have to go Garna by tonight's train; the job I've been wanting for the vacation has come through and won't wait unless I go at once. »

« But college, you won't get your credits if you leave now; it's almost a month before the end of the term », she replied.

« To the devil with college. Do I get anything out of it? It isn't me that expects benefit from that damned place. College ought to be done away with. If I'd take the professors at that place for examples of what learning and education does to a person... God save the king. Nope. I'll leave tonight. I'll get credits for the semester too. You watch me. »

His mother curled a Scotch lip into an expression

betwixt resignation, irritation, and humourous toleration. She'd become that way through the course of years and the upbringing of her litter.

He hustled down to the depot and purchased a ticket for the seven P. M. train to Garna, then navigated himself towards the university to instruct his instructors to see that his credits came through. It was early spring, and the campus is always flooded with girls in sport coats, coloured jerseys, and light frocks, in the early spring. Most of them he knew too well to be romantic about, but one doesn't want to cut off from the indifferent joy of casual campus philandering without a little farewell.

As soon he struck the walk leading from Museum Park to the Campus along came Margaret Geiss and Diana Lisbon. « My gad, Diana », he exclaimed, « I won't be able to take you to the dance Saturday night because I just received a telegram telling me to report on my summer's job at once. »

Diana received the news like a trojan. It was he who'd suffer, if either of them did, because of his not being able to take her to that dance. She didn't tilt dinky hats over her left eyebrow and swank about dressed up to the minute that was ten minutes ahead of the fashion because that was her only intention. After his airy and her airier regrets she went towards her car sitting out in front of the main college building ; and sat waiting for a conversation with whoever headed her way. It wasn't ten minutes later that he heard six fellows argueing with her that she ought to cut her French class and take them all for a ride around to the high-scool to show the infants there what grown up students look like.

His professors in Philosophy, economics, sociology and bionomics all agreed, not with so much enthusiasm as to add too much to his conceit, that he was sufficiently brilliant to be able to miss the last month in their courses without destruction of too much potential energy, that trained rightly in time, would make for general social welfare. They assured him that they'd put in passing standings at the registrar's office, and naively suggested that if he had time he could write papers on certain themes and mail to them.

His history professor caught a habituary hiccough in his throat, gulped on his Adam's apple for a minute or so, and stated « Actually you know... »

David couldn't wait for him to chew his reflections, and had no time to listen to his unoriginal ideas on scholarship, and thoroughness. « You shriveled up crabapple », he thought, and collected the many contempts in his nature into a manner of hauteur. « Do as you wish about my credit; I must go; I need the money from this position and it will not wait for me. If you wish to insist upon measuring information by the number of hours spent in the classroom it's not probable that our ideas on what's advantageous in education will ever meet anyway. » As David left him all the distastes for scholastic mentalities, catalogued information, and tremorous erudition, were belging up into the mouth of his consciousness. Going down the steps though he ran unto Virginia Yokes and Sally Murray, and remembered with a qualm that he was the only person — so they said — who knew they were contemplating an elopement with a couple of nineteen year old fellows who had jobs, itinerant he feared, with moving picture companies.

« Say Virg, for Pete's sake, I have to desert the ship and go down into the valley to watch over Mexican labourers who work on irrigation ditches. My last word of warning; for Lord's sake woman think a little bit backwards and remember that you've fallen in love with every half-respectable looking male who's treated you gently, and postpone marriage for a year or so. »

Virgie's spanish eyes fluttered as she looked at him with sidewise contemplative coquetry. She was too dusky a rose already to blush.

« I don't know what to do, but I can't stand college another year. »

« Well, if you do marry, be careful. A marriage can be wormed out of, but if you have an infant... »

Sally Murray lifted up her right foot to wipe dust off it on her left stocking. It was such habits of Sallie's which had driven Russell Simpson from infatuation to rapid disapproval of Sally. « She's a classy dresser and cute to look at, but she's too squirmy for me », he had remarked.

« Your dad has enough money so you won't suffer anyway », he commented to her. « Well, what to hell, I'll come back in the fall and find you at college whether you elope or not. You'll tire of marriage soon, both of you. I suppose it's as interesting an experience as any other, but you'd much better be reckless with conventions other than with marriage laws if certain impulses are too strong in you. »

He had to hurry on, so shook hands with and kissed Sally and Virg good bye, and ran on down the steps of the main college building, regretting the trivial but pleasurable hours of campus life he'd miss. At once he ran unto a group of fellows talking about the basketball finals. Amongst them were three of his fraternity brothers. After greeting them all, he asked his brethern to walk over to the house with him because he had to depart within a couple of hours to pack.

Burt Samuels untangled his long adolescent limbs from a bench and casting mooning eyes towards Virg, torn between two desires, of brotherly fellowship and of calflove, went with him. Jack and Bernard also loitered after. When they arrived at the house they found MacIntyre and Dr. Benjamin, respectively a « Greek » poet after the Keatsian manner of that greek condition, and a professor of English literature who clutched

youth by living in the fraternity house where much
of it abode. Immediately verbal warfare started
between Mac, the Doctor, and David. In the beginning they were defending tradition, rimed verse,
and college education; in the end no one knew
what they were defending.

« Abstract beauty rats ! » Hail to thee blithe
spirit, bird thou never wert.' Dave was saying after
getting well launched. « I wish you'd leave the
nightingales and roses alone for a while. It's
damned affectation ; a trance throwing. No man
ever thinks or feels his emotions in that way. You
(to MacIntyre), like Keats and Shelley, think it's
necessary to get upon some astral plane of poetic
emotion to write. Why can't you think and feel
directly and lend all the force of your intellectual-
emotional organism to perceiving rather than to the
trick of fooling yourself psychologically; I know a
man makes his own reality, but he can do so
rationally rather than resorting to the same sort of
emotional hysteria that negroes at an evangelistic
meeting do.

« I can tell you I write poetry on a par with
Theocritus and Homer », MacIntyre assured him.

« Who in hell thinks so but yourself ? What you
do is go out and have a love affair with some
blond waitress and because she let's you sleep
with her, you come back and write about her
immortal beauty. That'd go stronger with me if I
hadn't seen some of these immortal beauties you

indite your lines to ; and smelled them too. It'd be all right to make love poems about these beauties, I suppose — overdone I'd say — but the point is, you romantically lie to yourself about yourself and everything in life just as you do about the females who « inspire » your poems. Poetry is made out of the natural experience of life ; you don't have to seek a particular type of experience out of which to make art, and if you do, — well that's why you're no damned good.

Doctor Benjamin hemmed, and started : « The test is the intelligence of the trained sense of the judicious ». »

« Yep, and the test of intelligence is intelligence, so where are we now old top ? Simply because you don't want to stir your pedagogic mind to comprehend anything written later than 1890, and claim to like all the established classics, doesn't assure me that you have a trained sense », Dave answered him, and immediately after felt sorry, seeing the hurt look across his eyes, and knowing as he knew, that consciouness of failure, by all standards, intellectual, spiritual, and popular-economic, goaded the Doctor to bitterness and narrowness. During a lull in the discussion he observed the fleshy back of his yellow-haired head ; his big once–athletic frame ; his high forehead. He was a perverse mixture of brutishhess, fine sentiency, German sentimentalism, revolting spirit, and impulse to conform to middle class moralities.

An anxiousness to be away, and down at Garna, conversing with Paul Somerland, who had a job to fill, filled it competently, and who thought analytically rather than emotionally because of atmospheric pressure, took hold of Dave's mind. Not that he thought life remarkable, or reality at all beautiful, but a sickness of spirit possessed him on seeing the doctor, growing rapidly stolid and flabby both of body and mind, grasp so feverishly at youth by attempting to have its hilarity through indulging in its activities.

He said goodbye to all the fellows at the house, being rather distant to Mac and the Doctor. For the others he felt herd companionship, simply because they had no intellect, or pretense of intellectual interest that disagreed with his own.

Of course when he got home his mother had a few words of advice to give him too, telling him that after the summer he'd better start a law course, or even a course in medecine, to have some profession upon which to fall back in making a living.

« O the devil mother, lay off, leave me alone, leave me alone won't you ? I can't be a lawyer, or a doctor. Why do you insist to me so much on the common sense side of life ? Who can you point out to me who has « settled down sensibly », as you call it, that doesn't lead such a damned, dull, animal routine of an existence, that I'd want to shoot myself it I thought that was the end », he stormed.

« I'm only trying to help you. »

« Don't try to help me. You can't. I'm not a christian, don't give a damn about economic situation, don't want the stupid respect of people whose standards you want me to acquiesce to. I'm not the kind of being you are; you're not satisfied with the life you've lead yourself... why do you worry about me ? I'll find my own way, or it won't be found, and if it isn't it doesn't matter. You can't insure your children's futures. »

« Well, all right... but now you go to church on Sundays while in the valley. There's not so much to do down there that... »

« Go to church », he laughed, irritatedly. « I'll go to hell sure, mother, if I go to church. By the time I've listened to the cant that is preached in the pulpit I have enough resentment in my system to poison ten healthy souls, let alone my own. »

In his bedroom he bustled around packing a grip with some rough clothes for the summer's job, disgusted with himself for not being able to take his mother humourously, and for worrying her by argueing. « Damnfool to upset her. »

At seven he was at the depot and boarded the train, which pulled out within a few minutes. As the train rolled out into the country from Los Angelos so that he could see orange groves blossoming, palm trees stretching upward, a feeling of freedom came into me, and then one of melancholy. An abstract concept of the lightness, colour, and young exhuberance of college life — the brightness of coloured dresses worn by girls on the campus, the easy casual conversations of students strolling back and forth beneath the shade trees, cutting classes, going for auto rides; the affectionate dependent friendliness of Virg, Margaret, Diana, and of his fraternity brothers, — was in his mind, making him envious of their carefree quality. Still he realised that individually they were as little satisfied with existence as he was.

He began to look forward to seeing Paul Somerland again, telling himself that at last he'd be away from the provincialism of Californian mentalities for a time; away from the city where parents have made their money raising corn and hogs in Iowa, and from their offspring interested only in moving pictures, dress and owning an automobile. The city of sunshine, dancing and inanity... He wondered if Paul looked as much « like Jesus » as he'd looked two summers before, or if he had chopped off his bronze beard, or let the desert harden the soft look of patient understanding in his gentle eyes. What if his memory had played a trick on him as it had so often done, and he found Paul heavy and prejudiced ? He must earn much money this summer and get away from California, to New-York, to Europe — somewhere.

He crawled into his berth and after a time went to sleep. In a half dreaming state the plot of a miraculously beautiful story that he must write at once came into his mind but when he awoke and thought about it it seemed quite flat. So he went to sleep again. Upon awaking in the morning he looked out the window across stretches of desert towards a mountain range, dun, and violet, and luminously vapoured with the light of the on-coming sun.

It was but five o'clock yet he arose and dressed. Leaving his baggage on the platform of the depot he walked out into desert. Aware that nobody would be up in Garna, which was about a quarter of a mile back from the sidetrack upon which the sleeping car rested, he did not go in that direction; but struck out across the sand, simply to feel the clarity and cleanliness of the desert and of its dry air, still cool with night. An owl flew up in front of him and lighted some distance away; he walked towards it; it flew again and did this repeatedly. Many gazelle-like lizzards, bronze and gray, and moss-green, ran across the sands, stopping quickly to lift a forefoot and stand alertly listening. They were impossible to catch or to hit with a stone. Ahead of him at one time he saw a rattle snake resting stretched out on the sand. Picking up a long branch of mesquite wood he approached him. The snake rattled and jerked himself into a coil. David reached the long stick out towards him and he struck at it; and snapped back his striking head over his coil again. He struck again. At last David hit him, breaking his back, and then killed him at once, first battering his head with the stick, then grinding it into the sand with the heel of his boot.

The sun was all in view now ; plainly it was going to be a very hot day, well around 110 degrees, but with a dry heat that did not disturb him.

A quality of the desert was beautiful beyond the beauty of things more sensuous and colourful : The manner in which expanse of sand followed expanse of sand; clarity of sky rested upon clarity of sky, and only the seared colors, the ascetic colours of the desert blended into the dun stretches of sand; The dim lavender of desert flowers, the dusty gray of sagebrush, seared green of mesquite branch, and rusty red of its bean — block on block of tri-dimensional extension — impalpable plane of clarity intersecting impalpable plane of clarity — the desert gave more sense of structure and of foundation than the most carefully planned metropolis.

By seven thirty, he was hungry and knew that the Chink would be serving breakfast now. When he went into the restaurant old Charlie Ling was flapping around, serving breakfast to mexican labourers in the same Chinese slippers, and black slipover shirt that he'd worn two years before, it looked to David. It seemed that for a moment a light of recognition flickered in his apathetically placid face, but oriental contempt obliterated the light. Perhaps he remembered David, and rememb

ered also that he'd once said so that old Ling
heard, that this kitchen was so dirty it gave him
indigestion to be in it.

Eating ham and eggs with his face turned
toward the street window to be able to see anybody passing, he saw Paul going by and hailed
him. Paul came in, and assured David that there
was plenty of work for him to do, as the bi-annual
flood of the Colorado river was expected any day,
and he had nobody to act as foreman for one of
his Mexican gangs who were piling rock along the
banks of the levee to restrain the water when the
flood did strike.

As they talked, several ranchers who lived near
town and men who worked at the irrigation Company's office came in to breakfast. Soon the restaurant was filled with the sound of voices
argueing about the day of arrival for the flood,
the loss of cotton crops, the price of mushmelons,
the management of the water company, and the
proper way of controlling the flood. Two men
changed the conversation to national politics, one
of them strongly defending the administration of
President Wilson and his actions regarding the
League of Nations. As Paul was holding forth in a
condemnation of Wilson's policy, in a way that
indicated clearly what school of social change
journalism he followed, David reflected that he
had coarsened, both in physical appearance and
intellectually. He wondered if that was the inevit-

able attrition of an environment created by beings disturbed solely by the economic problems of life, or the settling of a naturally dogmatic organism into its mode of responding to life, once the inquisitive unrest of youth had left it.

Soon Paul and he went out on the street and down to the levee office together, and Paul began to tell of the engineering problems, and the political problems of his position.

« They 've placed a damned old fogey of an engineer on the district board, and he, partly out of ignorance, and partly to insure himself a job as assistant engineer — who ever heard of such a thing as being an employee authorised to spend money for a county, and also on the board which gives the authority? — he insists that a channel should be blasted to form a new river bed, and thus divert a part of the river stream. Utter damnfoolishness! Millions of dollars could be spent trying to blast a river bed down to the gulf of Mexico, some five hundred miles, and the next spring the river would resume its old course. »

« What should be done? » David asked.

« What we 're doing, though we have to battle old Woods and his followers continually. We' re blasting rock out at the various quarries along the course of the levee and piling a wall twelve feet through and fourteen feet high; and when flood waters hit that wall they won't break through. »

« Old Woods ! is that your competing engineer. I remember seeing that old bird when I was here two summers ago. He used to go out in the morning with helpers — that lame redheaded fellow who was drowned — and sit around in his boat somewhere in the Colorado river. Didn't give a damn where he blasted, so long as he had dynamite and blasted somewhere. Does anybody take him seriouly ? »

« Two-thirds of the valley think that I and my partner are young upstarts with newfangled notions who will bring destruction upon their cotton crops. All Woods wants is to secure a job for himself and his loafing friends. »

They turned into the levee office and Dave picked out a canteen, threw off his coat, and soon Paul and he were on their way out to where the Mexicans were piling rock, twelve miles from town. The Ford waded bravely through sand grooved a foot deep in some places by the passing of trucks.

« You don't know how glad I am to have you here ; I haven't talked to an intelligent person for six months, and don't have time to read the papers that are sent me from New-York », Paul assured David.

A quality of softness, and gentleness, that was in him seemed to battle with mercenary lusts, and a rough irritation directed consciously at the « ignorant brutes » who made up the populace of the valley, directed subconsciously at — him, Dave felt — or at anybody who had active and current cultural interests, since all his own energies were being utilized in the politics of his engineering position. His situation was beyond Dave's ability to think through. Such work as he was doing had to be done, he couldn't hold his position and devote half-interest to its problems. Inwardly David shrugged his shoulders : either he was too fine a being to be doing such work, and somebody else would doit, or he wasn't too fine and he would do the work and gradually cease to care about development other than material, important only to such people as demand something of life other than living.

In half an hours time, a respect and an affection that Dave cherished for him had evaporated so that he looked at and into him as much as he could, quite coldly and impersonally, noting that while the features of his profile were clean, the back of his head shot down with displeasing straightness ; that beneath the first impression of a « sweet jesus » quality was a more permanent one of harshness such as is found in Germans hospitable and kindly by tradition, rather than by nature.

It occured to David that Paul was shocked during the course of their conversation driving out to the levee by his saying that he thought patriotism a narrow ideal. « It's simply a group-selfish ideal, is entirely economic, and quite often places a high price on insincerity and inability to think. One is born of the country to which one is native and because of that, and its environment, possesses some of the general qualities of that country. Beyond that, race indicates little when it comes to the finest expression of human energy. Why should one sentimentalise to continue a prejudice ? The only ideal that is worth possessing is that of intelligence — more sentimental ideals have elements of the gross and evasive in them », he had said. Paul did not speak his dis-agreement.

It was evident that his attitude towards David was no longer one of personal affection, now ; rather an attitude of resentment. Not that any point upon which they might disagree mattered, or that Dave's seeming to have proved a point mattered. Paul was simply aware that regardless of the correctness of David's conclusion, he was less apt now to accept judgements because they were accepted than was he himself, and he was still sentient enough to desire to arrive at his own convictions.

He started talking of literature ; of the stage ; of politics ; David found his interest in what Paul knew of these things dead. So he asked questions about plans for the summer's work and Paul was soon talking entirely about the problem of levee construction and flood control.

« I've been wanting to put up a derrick with

which to handle stone too big for men to handle alone », he declared and drew a sketch of the derrick. « Do you think you could supervise its erection ? »

« Perhaps — explain it to me a little. »

It amazed and pleased David to find that he understood what Paul was saying when he did explain, because he'd been afraid that it was an involved engineering structure and that it would be necessary for him to look intelligent and say « yes, O yes » while comprehending nothing.

At last they reached a turn in the levee where some horses were tied to ropes between two poles. Paul stopped the car and they climbed out to walk down the levee together. « There's the Mexican foreman — he can't read or write well, but he has plenty of savee just the same », Paul remarked and called out :

« Harry — O Harry Gallego, come over here. » When Harry arrived, Paul introduced him to David and in a few minutes got into the Ford saying that he must get back to town and might not be able to be out again for a couple of days.

Harry and David took to each other easily. Two minutes after Paul had departed Harry was telling Dave about his plans for being a labour-contractor, and bidding for irrigation ditchcleaning, and brush-cutting jobs, to make big money.

« They ain't nothing to being a labour contractor

except a little adventuring spirit », he commented. « Me and my brother had a good start down at a mine in Arizona before the war and made some- times as much as a thousand dollars each a month... Do you keep books, and write checks? Maybe you and me could get together and be partners. »

« You try me kid. I can write cheeks and keep books all right. Start something and I'll be in with you up to my ears », Dave assured him.

« That's the boy. Do you drink — just a minute — keep this quiet though, don't let Mr. Somerland know I have any of this stuff on the job — try that — real fire water », he said, taking a bottle of whis- key from under a pile of sacks. « And don't you ever let nobody tell you that stuff's hard to get be- cause prohibition's on. As long as you're in this valley and stay in with me I'll see that you get all you want. »

David gulped at the fire water and it tickled him down to the toes.

« Watcha doing Saturday night? They's a dance on amongst us Mexicans — that's what I am, none of this Spanish stuff for me, I ain't a highbrow — I don't dance well and my wife likes to dance. She's a nice kid, more class than I got; used to be a stenographer before she married me. »

They arranged to go to the dance together Sat- urday night, as they walked down the Levee to- gether and Harry pointed out the labourers who were dependable workmen or who spoke English or who were « men to keep an eye on ». « It's hard keeping men on this job in weather that's up to 127 in the shade. »

« You can't blame them for not liking quarry work in such heat », David said.

Out across the desert for miles stretched innumerable rocky hills, from the nearer ones of which loads of stone appeared, the horses driven by negroes or Indians or Mexicans. « We'll take the two riding ponies and do the round of gangs so you'll know where all the men are working. If you do the rounds twice a day to take the men's time and give the gang bosses any help you can, there won't be much for you to do beyond that. You can make a little extra money keeping books for me, and making out my pay checks every two weeks if you want to », Harry said, as they mounted the ponies and started out.

Up through the rocky hills they rode, Harry a round-bodied jovial moonfaced man of a horseman, a kewpyish smile on his brown face as he chattered on. On a ways they ran into his brother Ginger, whose make up indicated a graver outlook on life and less alert precocity, but who neverthless, perhaps due to remarks Harry made to him in Spanish, began almost at once to tell David about his private business and family affairs. The Mexican labourers in his gang surveyed David. The Indian labourers seemed less curious about the new boss. They drove on. And in about an hours time were back at the starting point and resting on a pile of gunny sacks spread beneath a thatched roof on poles. As they half–dozed an auto drove into the stable yard and old Woods came up. He approached and began talking to Harry giving Dave a casual glance of curiosity. Dave knew that he did not .know him by sight, and remained silent for a bit listening to their conversation ?

« Jesus Christ, Harry, I'm getting too old to tear around on hot days like this », he exclaimed. He sat down, his broad bulky figure relaxing. For some seconds he gazed abstractedly off into space, like a dazed man trying to think what to think about. His watery–gray eyes had a dim glaze over them; his iron gray beard was clean, but neverthless it made one feel as old men's beards generally do — that in eating, foodstuffs and liquids would cling to it, that at any time it might be spotted with tobacco juice. The curled hair on his head clung to a well–formed, round type of dome. It struck Dave that Paul was too bitter about the old man, who could be manipulated rather than credited with sufficient force to merit direct opposition.

« The county ought to fix up them roads », he said after a time. « It has eft me with a pain in the loin driving out over them. Like leaving a woman half-screwed, I say it is, and that ain't considerate, is it ? » the old man broke into speach with again.

« Which is that harder on, the man or the woman », Dave asked him. He turned eyes of doubt on

Dave, his dignity perhaps a trifle upset to be addressed when they had not been introdueed.

« Who are you ? » he questioned directly ?

Harry introduced them saying that Dave was a boy from college here for the summer.

« What are you taking at college? » Woods inquired.

« Not much of it takes. I have a healthy system and throw that sort of thing off readily. I 've tried several things, economics under a scarecrow with a mania for statistics, sociology under a revitalized mummy with a theory that all branches of human knowledge can be ;card-indexed under eighty six heads with subheads, and philosophy under an ex–methodist minister suffering with a senile fear that he cannot justify his belief in God and the good, rationally. — O yes, I took a shot at psychology thinking I might be a psychoanalyst until I learned what types of beings I'd have to perform upon. »

Old Woods brightened up. Dave was aware at once that he might have made an error in showing him he possessed a wit, so that it would be harder to observe his specie through him in its ungarnished state. He'd concluded not to take either side in the controversy between Woods and Paul, not only because of insufficient knowledge to know the merits of their varying theories, but because Woods seemed as interesting a type as Paul, and with less intense social conscience.

¿ « What is that stuff psychoanalysis ! I 've heard it mentioned and thought maybe I was getting behind the times », Woods said.

« Perhaps you 'll be ahead of them by knowing nothing about it. Apart from several schools, it is the analysis of motives, subsconcious, and conscious, of human organisms. You've probably been hearing about it in connection with dream-analysis, which aims to discover the type of desires suppressed, and impulses in, any subject analyzed, through their dreams... Not unnaturally the desires are generally found to tie up in some way with sex... »

« That thing sex is important, isn't it », he chuckled.

« Yes, and about one-tenth understood. It's rather too bad that psychoanalysis should have become a subject for popular discussion since the average being can't think of sexual desire except in terms of the physically voluptuous. The factors of intellect, and a complex social organisation which creates desire for social power, acclaim, and intercourse which permits communion on a basis of understanding, complicate any impulse so that fleshly solutions are insufficiently perceptive », Dave told Woods, aware that he did not understand much of what was being said, and amused at both Woods' bafflement and his own grandiloquence.

« That's so; that's so; I've always said you can't know too much about sex. Now you take the

flowers; even they smell sweetest at the moment
of copulation — you know flowers copulate —
that is they do, don't they ? » Woods started off, at
first to inform Dave, then recalling that his information might be *passé*; of a generation forty years
back, then turning in his mind to consult David.

However instead of going into this theme, David
went on with his. « It's probably society as a whole
that needs to be psychoanalyzed rather than individuals, because there is certainly vicious suppres-
sion in any social organism which expresses itself
consciously in such conventions and moralities as
deny the cleanness or at least the presence of natural impulses, and place a premium upon ignorance
and unvirility. »

« You're quite a bolshevik, ain't you ? » Woods
asked and went on, « that's the thing for the young
generation to be. »

« No, not a bolshevist or a socialist, or a com-
munist, politically not much of anything but a
spectator. Change occurs because of the strongest
force, generally that of the aggressive minority
rather than of either the majority or of the intelligent few. I'm sure that communism would
oppress sensitive beings, artists, scientists, and
people who want a morality higher than the economic, quite as much as the present system of
Government. There is more oppression in narrow
moralities than there is in economic or political
situation. I don't mind not eating now and then,

but I do mind not being able to say what I sincerely feel and think because of coventional attitudes. Not having any assurance of intelligence amongst the greater portion of humanity, one man or group, can never know how any ideal social system will work out — anyway I'm not one of the types of beings hopeful enough to devote my direct energies to battling for an ideal societary system. »

Old man Woods went off into a mood of abstraction that might have meant deep thought, but which David suspected was the dazed idealess reflection of a man given to apathetic trances. The day was too hot for continued speach and drowsy with late afternoon. After a time he looked alert again, and Dave was aware that he was looking him over.

« You have an intellect, my boy », he started.

« No, no, no, please! That remark would have pleased me once, and it may again, but for the time being, I'm sick of intellect, it doesn't mean sense. I know I'm strong on ideation, but that does'nt mean I'm intelligent enough to be mentally and emotionally adjusted. »

Conversation stopped again, with old Woods going off into another dazed trance. After a time he stated that he'd have to start back to town and walked off absent-mindedly.

« Takes coke, doesn't he ? » David asked Harry.

« I don't know. It ain't liquor that makes him that way. Mr. Somerland would have liked to hear

you say that. Them two ain't friends at all »
Harry said.

« I rather believe that the old man is the wiser of
the two by nature but he probably isn't much of
an engineer », Dave murmured, reflecting on the
states of mankind, and growing no wiser because
of that reflection.

« He may be getting too much bumping from
that widow Brown he knows, Harry said, or
just getting stupid from sitting around on his ass
too much. That's the only thing I've ever seen
him do. »

It was quitting time, and the labourers came
walking up the levee to get into the trucks and be
driven to town. Harry and Dave sat in the seat of
one truck and Harry's brother came in one behind
them. In an hour they were all at Garna.

« Come on over to the shanty pool hall with me
and have a drink. Old Joe wouldn't give it to you
alone. I'll introduce you so you can get it after this,
by yourself », Harry said to Dave.

A fat, greasy-faced Mexican in sloppy trousers
and a dirty shirt that was open all the way down
the front, so that the tip of his belly-button showed,
was sitting out in front of the adobe–hut poolhall.
With a grunt he lead Dave and Harry into a back
room and served them, then departed, leaving them
sitting at a wood box for a table, But they soon
finished their whiskeys and left the pool hall and
each other, David going to a negro restaurant

which he thought cleaner than Charlie Ling's.

The old mammy who ran the place recognized him and was vociferous in her greetings. «Us cullud folks in the valley has been getting religion this summer ; and they ain't no more bawdy girls amongst us. Down whah we lives we holds evan‑gelical meetings nights now instead of actin «rowdy», she told David, but he wasn't sure she was as pleased about that as she might have been, because later remarks of hers about the cullud minister were disparaging.

«He's a God-fearing man, but he has his hungers. Lawdy land how that niggah can eat. He remarks to Sister Beachum that «ah can't preach heah on earth and board in heaven : the word of God ain't dissembled gratis», and she told him to eat at her place, Mah goodness, she didn't know how he can eat. »

After Dave had eaten he went out into the street and saw Paul coming down the one street of the town, with several other men. Paul separated and joined David. He, immediately began to talk about national politics.

«I've ceased to expect much from either political or social systems, Dave said », realization of value is individual rather than group — O perhaps a little rope; the majority are tied to a stake — their material hungers — and they wind up their own tether rope, so that they have less space to circle about in sometimes than others.

« That's simply a lazy mental attitude », Paul responded.

« Hardly that : it doesn't say you don't work mentally in striving to understand, relate, and as an individual use, what experience existence thrusts in your way. »

« Selfish egoism. »

« What's humanitarianism but the generalizing of your own self-pity. Nothing solved by sentimentality. One might as well try to have as hard an intelligence as the force which casts events is hard.

« What does one do ? »

« Solve one's own difficulties, and the difficulties of such as around you as you can help. The application of an inclusive social, political, or religious, ideal plays the hell in general, as bigoted morality now oppresses America and England — well — if it is n't puritan narrowness however, it's something else. All solutions of life are individual. That's not selfishness in any material sense; it's recognition of the limitations of human intelligence. »

David felt a restless irritation in himself ; a desire to be away from Paul and not discussing social theory. Soon he excused himself to « write letters » and went to his room in a shack that lay just on the edge of a stretch of desert, across which, a quarter of a mile away lay the negro village that two years before had been a redlight section.

The day was an coal ember from which the fire

was departing in the cooler vapours of evening. Mist veiled the dry clarity and coloured mist — pale lavender, dim prismatic — colours, curled around the bodies of the mountains that cut off a view of the horizon on a level. Already, voices, the strumming of banjos and other musical instruments came sounding from the negro village. The mellow voice of some darky shouting at his horses as he was unharnessing them after a day's work ; the friendly bark of dogs ; the calling of a female voice across some backyard to a neighbour ; curses, laughter, came across the stretch of sand intensifying the quietude and tranquillity that David felt about him. No sweeter odour than the odourlessness about him, no sweeter music than the punctuated silences — it seemed to David that his spirit, his mind, his body, had been being racked and tormented for years, but that now, here, he could rest, and think thoughts that did not turn upon him to wound him with irritation, insistent upon the stupidities and oppressions that are everywhere in the world.

The sense that he had gotten in the morning of the structural solidity of the desert was increased, but with the increase came a feeling of the suavity of its structural simplicity; the plastic invisibility of the ozoneous sky, darkening now, erected upon this vastness of sand. Space is a monument carved with utmost simplicity.

Night decreased his world, and increased his

comfort since he rested snugly in a cleanly
dark portion of a valley enclosed in mountains.
Memory was with him : Yes outside there were
cities, throngs of people, a cosmopolitan world.
They had always been hovering around the
unreality for him; they were now, dim, distant, completely without reality, even that of a
dream. Ideas that were wont to taunt him — of
achievement, of lust, — unrestful, self-accusing
ideas — discontent with environment, with social
systems — all had become so meaninglessly unreal.
He stood for a time at the doorway of his shack,
shirtless because much heat was still in the
evening air. It rather surprised him when his
hands touched the flesh of his own arms as he put
them akimbo. Even his own body had partaken of
unreality. Not a happy feeling within him; not an
unhappy one; only one utterly quiescent.

Now the sound of many negroes chanting, and
praying, came intermittently to him; space, and
tiny gusts of breeze acting like stop valves to shut
off the echoes, then re-opening them to let the
contralto, burnt-orange tones of melodious mourn-
ful voices come into his ear.

Velvet-clad hoofs, tiny and exquisitely wrought,
were pacing on bronze stairways, making music
as they loped on the ascending plains of moonbeams up the sky, startled antelope with slender
necks and gracile erect antlers were lifting neat
heads upon lithe undulant necks, as they listened

with ruby-bright gleaming eyes, before darting upward and away through the veils of yellow gleaming in the musky glow of desert night; the desert an ember within which vermillion heat still burned inside the ashy exterior of darkness.

He put a shirt on, and stepped out into the sand to walk nearer to the negro village so that he could hear them in their religious rites. Arriving outside the tumble down shack in which the ceremony was being held — a shack held together with poles, boards, and covered scantily with dirty canvass — he stood looking in through the doorless doorway.

A woman was talking. As she talked other voices, spoke reverently, in fatherly tones, in patronizingly motherly tones saying, « O Lord » « Heah the woman Jesus » « She's yours God ». Her words came to his ears :

« It ain't as if ah was advisin' you Lawd, ah's youah servant lawd, an what you see fitten for me to have ah has and is radiant wif joy; but ah's askin you to be wif me, caus the serpent of sin is around me lawd, urging me to be bad lik ah has always been befoah you glohaified me. And the way of the serpent is calculated to git around me and drag me back into sin. He ain't like de snakes out heah on dis heah desert. He's sociable and when he talks, he talks like he talked to dat woman Eve and his voice is sweeter dan honey — Ooooooooh Lawd, be wif me. It ain't like I hadn't been a wicked woman and knows de pleasures of de flesh ; it ain't like dreams don't come to me, and when dey comes dat de serpent ain't dey askin' me to come and lie wif him in de shape of man. O lawd ; O blessed Jesus, you's mah man now ; ah's all yoah's Jesus, all yoah's. »

As the woman continued speaking her voice rose to shrillness and took on all the volume of which it was capable until her talking was a incoherent stream of hysterical shrieking, she beat her bosom and ran her hands through her hair. At last she stopped and after a deep male voice had said

« O help her Jesus. »

There was silence for a moment or so, until all the darkies took up a spoken song ; that swung into a chant, beat with rhythm, and became fervourous. David walked away from the shack in which the black people were sitting, towards that of his own room. Moonbeams were running in streams up the sky. Making the night to effervesce, electric with soft vitality ; as champagne which is charged with a steady current as it bubbles.

The next day David was out at the levee with the labouring gang by seven thirty. Even days of unremarkable events followed each other, but hot, mistlessly clear days, which in the early morning were aggressive with clarity as though innumerable bright flowers were being thrown into the air, so that their petals were fluttering about, petal on petal of clarity, falling, floating, keeping the air bright and scentless of all scents but that of spaceousness. Later in the day, the heat brought a consciousness of intensity brooding somewhere in the infinity of sky, and of a red glow gleaming hotly through the opaque petals of clarity.

During the day sometimes Mexican and Indian labourers would strip, while waiting for a wagon of rocks to come along to be piled along the banks of the levee. Then they would jump into the silty, clay red-hued water from the Colorado river to cool of and splash about, their luminous-skinned bodies gleaming where portions of them showed above the satin rustiness of the flowing water.

Somedays old man Woods, or Paul, would come out and spend an hour or so. Davis would exchange desultory conversation with Paul, habitually friendly. With old man Woods he would converse with seriousness upon problems of the universe, life, religion, sex, botany, or men.

« I tell you the flood's going to break that damn; them engineers won't stop it with rocks, and besides they didn't start piling rocks soon enough to have a bank sufficient before the flood hits the levee banks », Woods said one day.

David believed that he was right, simply because an instinct of inevitability was in him, not because of belief in the old man's judgement. The flood breaking would be an economic fatality for some

in the valley; loss of property and of cotton and
melon crops. It seemed to him hardly worth
attempting to forestall fatalities, but that this was
the way to do, go on working doggedly and expect
what you wish but accept what comes.

Saturday nights Harry would take him to a
dance in some Mexican hall, and they would stand
around, drinking wine or beer, and conversing
with other men. Generally Harry's wife would be
there in a black velvet dress, cut low at the neck so
that her orange white flesh gleamed erectly above
it. Other Mexican girls were there sitting along
the sides of the walls waiting to be asked to dance;
but few of them were asked and would dance
with each other. There were only two of nearly
twenty of them who were good looking and they
were so surrounded by Mexican swains that David
despaired of dancing with them often and would
take on Harry's wife or Harry's sister-in-law, a
huge woman in a green plush and embroidered
dress — of material like chair upholstery. She
could not dance, so he would simply keep his feet
out of her way and smile and talk; and lead her to
her seat at the end of the dance thankful that it
was over and feeling very generous within himself
for his philanthropic nature. Harry's wife was a
different story, but David suspected that Harry
wasn't keen on having him dance too often with
her, because he'd remark :

« My wife 's some kid aint' she ? You like her I

guess. It's a fact, she 's classier that I am. I ain't had much schooling. »

One night there was a negro barbecue and dance on in town, and David could get no one who would go with him. Paul was busy; Harry had to stay with his wife and children; others were afraid that the party would get too rough with some razor using; and perhaps resentment on the part of some of the negroes towards white men. However David managed to get to the dance hall at about eleven o'clock at night after the barbecue feast had been held on the outskirts of town and the negroes had left the remnants of food, canteloupes, pieces of roast chicken, corn fritters, and half empty beer bottles, strewn about where the central fire had been blazing. Many of the older coloured people had retired to their homes, and only the gay bucks and maidens had come to the dance hall in numbers at all, though some old mammies and gray-headed males were sitting around with wistful shining black faces as they listened to the music tapping their feet or shrugging their shoulders in rhythm.

David came to the door of the dance hall and looked on. After a time he stepped inside and stood near the door watching. There were no other white men about. One or two Mexicans, and over in a corner an Indian girl, a flabby, early matron-ized body she had, were watching proceedings with desiring, yet apathetic eyes.

In the orchestra was a violonist who swayed and rocked and shouted out like a dog howling at the moon frequently, a pianist who bounced up and down on the piano stool as he played, doing dance steps with his feet, wiggling his shoulders; and a drummer who beat his drum madly, banging his bass and snare drums, and all their metal contraptions with inspirational bang and excited enthusiam. Now and then he would grab a potato whistle and make yodeling, minor, shrieking, calliope noises. Shouts and half-started melodies came from all over the room, particularly from the young bucks dancing with the dusky-skinned charmers. The scene was too openly an intoxication of sensuousness to be lascivious or obscene.

After a time however David found the flesh-odour in the room, the smokiness, and closeness, irritating and oppressing, so he went out, and back to his shack to sleep. As he was starting down the street a young negress accosted him. saying: « Hey thah Honey, whah's you goin ? Doan you want company ? » He laughed, looking at her dubiously. « No, I think not, hardly worth the chances » he replied, thinking that if it weren't for the smallness of the town and the way stories spread he wouldn't be so sure.

The water has risen twelve inches during the night, and already for the last four days every rancher in the valley who could possibly get away

from his work was working on the levee, bringing
with him from home all the gunnysacks he could,
to fill with sand and pile up along the banks to
restrain the flood waters. During rest periods some
of the ranchers could be heard complaining
because this or that other rancher hadn't arrived.
« He won't have any crop to work on if the flood
breaks. This is a community matter, but you can
trust that man to always let somebody else do his
civic work for him » they'd complain.

Other men would boast that they hadn't slept
for twenty-four, or for thirty-six hours, but had
piled sacks at leakholes, or had carried coffee
around to the men. Everywhere was a great dis-
regard for all the ordinary routines of living.
Everywhere were men pumped full with excitement and consciousness of their own necessity in
this crisis. Whenever any one of them stopped to
talk, he always was just resting a bit and had to
rush back to work immediately to direct the
Mexicans, or the other ranchers who were less
efficient and able to see just what spots to pile
sandbags on, than was he. There wasn't a man on
the job who did not know that if the flood was
diverted, it would be because of something he had
advised or supervised, and that if the flood broke
that it was because somebody else had failed to
follow his directions.

Back some ways from the levee banks, several
thatch roofed shacks stood, speedily erected to

serve as kitchen roofs, under which cooking might be done, and men served meals. The ground about the place had begun, in the last few days, to be soggy with water that was coming up from underneath because of the flood water pressure. Not more than 50 feet from the kitchen all of the horses were fastened to a line of poles, and there they were fed. That same line of poles had served for years as the stable for horses hauling for labouring gangs who worked about the levee, in consequence of which all the ground about was covered with manure so that when the water had dampened it, ammoniacal odours arose in the air and permeated the whole atmosphere near the kitchen.

Several cooks were employed about the place. One horribly dirty Mexican with a screw fastened into a wooden stump serving as one arm; another, an old Scotchman with a cross dog disposition, the sort of man who has led a precarious life, isolated from ordinarily decent human contacts. Still others, waiters, kitchen boys, assistant cooks were about the place, cursing and reviling each other, the men at work for their carelessness and for their appetites, and the location for its uncleanness. The management of the water company came in for its curses too, for not being prepared in case of such emergencies, and for rushing out such stoves and such equipment as though it were possible to prepare food fit for humans to eat with such a layout:

If the Mexican cook ever washed his hands no one saw him. He would go about bare-armed, from kneading dough for pies or biscuits, to rolling lumps of ground meat into loaves. Stopping sometimes, he would step not far to the side of the kitchen to excrete his organs, which function being performed; he would return to work, stolidly and sullenly. To exaggerate the condition, millions of flies were about every pot on the stove, every can of fruit, bit of pastry, barrels of sugar, and during meal times were in swarms about the foods on the table. Many men could scarcely eat because of the flies in the cooking, and the flies swarming about their heads. Others ate on indifferently, remarking : « This ain't no time to be delicate. »

David could not eat; before coming out in the morning he'd stop at a restaurant in town and eat; and have nothing more until the next morning. He'd discovered that a cook shack lay down the levee in which a crabbed old Irishman worked, placed there permanently, to have food on hand for any of the executives or engineers who were held on the job over meal times throughout the spring, summer and fall months. However, he discovered also, after having eaten one meal there, that this old man's habits of cooking were as unclean as the Mexican's at the major kitchen. Now the shack that he was in was surrounded by water — it was built upon a foundation of driven

piles and stood above the water generally, just off
the levee banks. The old man had always thrown
his food leavings out of the shackhouse door into
the water, and it stayed in the vicinity of the
shack, because of water brush that would not let
it float away on the stagnant, almost motionless
water. Occasionally now that the flood was on the
old man would jump into the water from the
shacksteps and with a broom brush back the slops
toward the open bay. Then he would climb out
and let the sun dry his clothes, which were never
changed. So David gave up the idea of eating
through the day.

Through the twenty four hours of night and
day, automobiles, trucks, horse–dragged wagons
were coming and going with loads of men, loads
of cement lime, loads of gunny sacks. The heat
was intense. The rising flood waters had put a
humidity into the air so that it was stifling to
breathe. Heat and humidity were circling, coiling,
writhing, and laying oppressive vapours upon the
lungs of everybody. Horses dropped in their
harness, men felt sick at stomach, and rested in
what shade they could find. But the water was still
rising.

David had been up till two or three in the
morning every day for the last week. He would
retire at 3 A. M., and get up again at seven to go
back on the job, rushing back and forth to keep
the various gangs supplied with sacks and men

more needed in one place than in another.

At about noon of this day the ranchers and the engineers began to feel that the crisis was past, and many of the ranchers departed for home so all gangs worked in a more desultory manner. On a corner, an intersection of a diverting levee channel, the main supply shack was situated; and David was sitting on a pile of gunnysacks chewing on a ham sandwich. Down the levee about an eight of a mile away some twenty Mexicans weere working without energy. Suddenly a shouting began. It increased and became hysterical and terrified. David jumped up. A moment later he heard a great rush of water. The levee had burst. In fifteen minutes acres about were being flooded, and the water kept pouring on. There was no way of stopping it now; only the subsiding of the flood would halt the continual pour of water down upon cotton crops, into stockfields, and around ranch-houses so that families would have to move back, taking their stock and carrying what machinery they could.

The rush of water, which would have sucked under any man attempting to swim across it, shut off all the twenty labourers who had been working down on a levee, so that they were stranded there as on an island. Some of them were shouting to be rescued, much afraid, but after a while others had assured them that they were safe as the levee ran for miles back. Only they were shut off from food and might have to sleep on the levee banks that night.

However David knew that they were all being hysterical and were quite safe, only the sight of the rush of water, swirling in whirlpools through the break in the levee frightened them — all illiterate Indians and Mexicans; with perhaps one or two white men of a poor sort who liked the importance of being appealed to by the others. In fifteen minutes after the water had broken through the entire gang was standing about calmly, smoking cigarettes, talking, feeling at ease almost now because the flood waters had made a decision and the work of piling rock and sandbags along the levee was over for the summer which would put them all out of a job.

Knowing that down the levee in the opposite direction on his side of the break, was a cookhouse, near which a boat was moored, David went in that direction, and arriving there jumped into the boat and pushed off. He intended rowing through the backwater bay, under the cottonwood brush to get to the men. Then they could all row back and forth across the break, upon water that was gaining a level as it poured through the break, a torrenting falls at first.

He got well out into the backwater bay, and had to bend his head and back and propel his boat forward by pushing against the thin trunks of trees growing out of the water, because the

brushwood leaning over him, and the cotton-
brush trees about him did not permit his sitting
upright, or his rowing. After five minutes of this,
he was as wet with perspiration as if he had jumped into the water. Around him on all sides now,
and overhead, was the crisp foliage of the cotton
brush, the leaves of which were covered with cobwebs and with cotton wool caused by the bursting
of the seed-pods of the trees. He could feel cobwebs
in his lungs, they were tangled up in his tongue
so that he must chew at them and gulp at them.
The atmosphere was smothering under all this
brushwood, and his breath was coming in ink-
tasting gasps. He cursed himself as a damnfool for
coming under swampy, sweating foliage, through
which he could not see to know what direction he
was going, forward or backward, or out away
from the levee. Waves of despair were going
through him; the only thing that made him go on
was the stifling oppressiveness of the atmosphere.

After what seemed to him an interminable time;
he saw a clearing and headed towards it. Arriving
at it, he saw the gang of men not far away and
rowed to them. « Before I'd do that again you
could sleep on the levee for three nights running »,
he commented as he came up. After resting for
about a quarter of an hour to get to breathing
naturally again he jumped into the levee water
and let the current carry him down the stream. It
sucked him under once, and held him sufficient

time for him to think thoughts of drowning and of self condemnation, and realization that he might as well have gone across in the boat, and have cooled off in the stiller waters on the other side of the break. However he came to the surface again, was whirled in several whirlpools of water for a minute or so and then thrown out by the current into water that he could direct himself in by swimming strokes. So he regained the levee bank on the other side and crawled out to shake the water off him a bit and dry a trifle before he climbed into an automobile to be driven back to town.

The next day men were standing around town talking about the flood, boasting of the work they'd done, each one saying his reasons why the thing had happened, and wouldn't have happened if.

Within a week a routine of existence more stale and oppressive than the breezeless weather had asserted itself. The streets of the town during the daytime were deserted, only an occasional woman would drive up in a buggy to the town grocery store, a cloud of silt dust subsiding behind her buggy. A man or woman would come out of the town bank, or the newspaper office, or the postoffice and disappear soon, into another door — to get a soda water or ice cream — or down the street towards home. Some dogs dragged heat-worn bodies from one shady spot to another, irritated at the sun's having disturbed their unrest-

ful doze. David knew that now his job was only a
pretence since most of the Mexican and Indian
labourers had been discharged or had quit and all
work was subsiding for the hottest months.

Soon, in the levee ditches, where the water had
been sixteen feet high it had sunk to four feet, and
the water lay stagnant and ill-smelling in the
bottom of the ditch. So little water was there now
that ranchers were continualy howling about not
having the water they needed for the irrigation of
their crops, much fewer of which were destroyed
by the flood than David had expected would be.

Through the drag of the days and nights David
became acquainted with most of the people in
town, and heard them chewing and re-chewing old
rags of conversation — exchange of criticism of
the water company management; of the inefficiency
of such and such a person; the insinuation that
another such and such a man was seen at the negro
section of town more than looked right. — He was
stiffling with the same comments on the same
flirtatious banker's daughter, the same uncareful
Mrs. Goldie — who had no last name; fifty times in
the course of the week he listened to Paul Somerland criticizing the theories of old man Woods;
sixty times a week he listened to other people cri-
ticising Paul; and when aiming at amiability or
graciousness the repertoire of entertaining conversation of the goodly valley inhabitants was yet
more limited.

One day Harry Gallego came up to David and told him that he was driving through the desert to Los Angeles, and that soon he'd drive to Fresno and contract some grape-picking jobs, as there would be nothing further doing in the valley till late fall. He wanted Dave to come along, rather afraid of doing the ninety miles of desert in which there was not an inhabitant alone. David agreed to go and upon telling Paul, found him rather relieved to have him quit the job though his manner was regretful. The situation in which Paul found himself after three years away from any life but the kind lived in the valley appalled David; he felt angry at himself for not being able to in some way halt the circumstances that were making a mere human animal of Paul. He could not, however, so he said goodbye and that night started off in an automobile across the desert. As they were leaving town they passed old man Woods, who, after some parley, decided to come with them, just as he was in a flannel shirt with his coat thrown over his arm. So he got into the car and on they drove.

They had been driving along, well away from town, and in sight only of desert stretches unplant-ed, before much talking was done. Harry drove the car, and he would chatter on a bit getting answers of abruptness. Old man Woods was in one of his abstracted contemplative moods, and David's ind mwas filled with schemes and plans about his activities when he got back to Los Angeles. Finally, perhaps because of the cooling evening air, and the sweet odourlessness of the space extending upward and out all ways from them, old man Woods began to liven up and then to speak.

« The older I get, the more of a pantheist I become; and it's bare places, or places away from men that make me feel the oneness of force in all nature. On the ocean too, as well as here on the desert — my mind struggles to think that infinity is really small, and that I'm puzzled about things in it only because my senses can't reach out enough to see, hear, and feel the edges of the universal complements of all my possible experience », he said to David.

David watched the old man's face whimsically, as he was speaking. « Does the idea of death disturb you; or have you always felt that way about the universe? There's a potential mysticism in us all but your processes had struck me as rational rather than as inspirational », he asked Woods.

« Worry me — death — I don't know. I don't know, boy, what I think or feel about it », Woods answered, then he chuckled. « You're meaning to suggest to me that I'm getting into my dotage aren't you? »

« No, no, no at all, I simply know that older people, men particularly, after the turmoil of 'succeeding in life' quite often relax, and decide because they as individuals can't govern events much », David commenced.

« As they can't when they're younger either », Woods interrupted.

« No, but one doesn't understand any better by believing because hungers in one makes one desire to believe. Religions are so often but a rationalization of primitive fears ; the savages with their animisms, fetishisms, and superstitions, aren't so very far behind many of us — there's mystery enough about us all right — our wills are limited in their ability to achieve — nevertheless there's no use in adding to universal mystery by a more finite variety easily explainable by psychology », David answered.

« What are you going to be after you're through college ? » Woods inquired.

« There I 'm more fatalistic than you I guess. I 'm going to be as rational as possible, then what degree of understanding — intelligence — that I possess will discover for me what to be... Now, I don't know. »

« Ah, but you're ambitious, aren't you ? »

David laughed reflectively. « Ambitious — for what ? I 'm not past adolescence yet. The only ambition I have is to understand, to be able to accept reality instead of try to recreate the universe continually, because romantic impulses in me rebel against the type of experience it inflicts upon me... I'm afraid of ambition a little, I believe, because I've known too many men, commercial giants mostly, since this is America, who had ambition, for power. How utterly tired they leave me, and hopeless, these Napoleons of finance; the individual Napoleon strikes me as stupid and insensitive. If there's nothing finer than that, the whole process of life is a miserably futile one. »

Harry broke into the conversation. « But say, the guy Napoleon was some man. He's the only person in that school thing, history, that I take my hat off to. That boy had a brain. »

« Maybe a brain's not enough. I don't know which is the worst fanaticism, mental or emotional. Military genius feeds no spirit. »

« You're one of these dreaming poetical fellows. The world's got to be fed, hasn't it ? » Harry responded.

« Has it been any better fed or any happier because of Napoleon, or of various commercial geniuses, or do these ' brainy ' men get much satisfaction out of existence themselves finally... Don't be sure I'm dreamy. The moon does'nt get too much attention from me; neither does sentimental romance nor love. If you were listening to Somerland and me the other day you'll remember that it wasnt' I who was feverish about retaining the ideal of patriotism. Don't be so sure that your own admiration of Napoleon isn't a dreamy ideal· There's a harder, more inevitable force than any military force that ever he could assemble. Why

rate human life and material as inventoried
stock ? »

Harry looked perplexed, and nothing more was
said, as David was watching his face, and recalled
what a ready-made sort of existence Harry had
had to live, amongst mines, working at day labour
from the time he was a boy. The night was as dark
as it would be, for it was about ten o'clock by now.
Still it was possible to see the desert ahead and
around them for an indefinite distance since
there were no distinguishing features to mark off
the space. The grey sheen of desert night through
which moonlight and starlight filtered was about
them as they rode on. Complete quietness and
tranquility was everywhere. The heavy breathing
of old man Woods emphasized the tranquillity.
David wondered if he was dozing, or simply brooding in an apathetic wonderment at life.

They went along without speaking for almost an
hour until Harry remarked that the car's radiator
was about out of water. « We'll soon be at Skinn-
er's well though and can get some water there. »

When the car came along the roadside entry to a
shack-house near which stood a well, placed in the
desert by a man who'd lived there alone for a time,
but who had now been gone for several years,
Harry stopped the car, and he and David went
over to the well. There was not a pail around and
not a rope to cast into the well; only a barbed
wire of great length, that was bent and twisted

however, so that it was impossible to manipulate in a manner to sink a little pail they'd taken from the car into the water of the well.

The well was sunk some five hundred to a thousand feet into the sand. Looking down, it was possible to see a little glimmer, perhaps water, perhaps mud. The dim suggestion of star reflection looked up. Down the side of the well was a ladder that went all of the way down to the water, it appeared so far as they could judge.

« We have to get water someway. Cars don't pass by this desert for days at a time, and when the heat comes on to-morrow we'll choke with thirst if we're stuck here... I guess we hadn't better take a chance though on having one of us climb down that ladder for water. That's a long climb : the steps may not be solid now, and it'll be suffocating down there », Harry said.

David stood over the well looking down, and rying to make himself think that they were in a perilous predicament. He could not however. The night was too gentle, tranquil, and unthreatening. He could look into the well, somewhat mystified in his senses, for it seemed strange that out here forty miles from any human settlement so well sunk and built a housing arrangement as this shack existed since there were no evidences about of mining or of agricultural opportunities.

« The man who had this dug and lived here must have been a queer sort », he commented.

After trying for a time to jerk the barbed wire about so that the pail fastened to the end of it would sink into the water far below they concluded that if it did strike the water and sink the pail, the distance they'd have to draw it up with the unwieldy wire would prevent the pail getting to the top with any water in it.

« I tell you, Harry said : I have to empty my bladder anyway. Do you? »

So they went back to the car, and told old man Woods that they'd have to drive on and take a chance on making the next thirty miles, to country where a few ranchers lived, and if the water in the radiator didn't last till then they were up against it. So after the three of them had urinated into the water tank of the car, they climbed in and drove on. Within half an hour they passed an intersecting road, and stopped. Dave went down it and after a ten minutes walk came to a house, which he discovered to be deserted after shouting about for some time. Off to the side of it however was a stock watering tank and in it was a little water covered with green stagnancy. Beneath the green stagnant mosses was sufficient water to fill the tank of the car, so he had Harry drive to the tank and after they had filled the car, and each drank a little of the water, they drove on, and inside of another hour had come to a district where little towns lay from ten to twenty miles apart. Beyond the first town a range of rocky hills lay, and turning the corner beyond one hill they came to a rock over which spring water was falling into a rock basin. There they stopped and lieing down in the sand, after drinking, they slept for some hours, until the morning sun woke them as it drove away the rock-shadow that protected them.

By twelve o'clock noon, they were in Los Angeles, and separated, David departing for home, after he'd made arrangements with Harry to go down to a Mexican bar to sit around and drink beer in the evening. Old man Woods was non-committal, declaring that he'd have to go back to Garna the next¦ day after he'd attended to a little business. « He probably has a woman in town, or has come to replenish his stock of dope, or of whisky », Harry suggested.

« Something like that I suppose. It doesn't matter. I have no curiosity about how the old man will spend his time here, or his remaining years. »

Arriving at home David greeted his mother, who, remarked when she had kissed him: « Home again ? They always come back sooner or later », and a little later was talking about what David had better take up at college the coming semester.

« Let the subject of college rest, mother. I'm not going back. There's nothing I could ever do with a degree because I shan't live the kind of life in which such letters signify. »

« What then — you can't drift forever. »

« No? — Well probably not. But I'll be leaving

for New-York or Mexico, or China or South America
— leaving for somewhere within the next week. »

His mother looked unsatisfied, then resigned.

« You will go your own way; that's all right
too. I guess everybody must be their own salvation,
but you won't find what you're looking for in any
of these out of the way places. You might just as
well settle here. »

« I might just as well not, too », David answered
ironically. « So that's that. You just leave my
generation's problems to be solved by the members
of that generation. »

« You want something to eat, I suppose. I'll see
what I can fix up for you », his mother parried, and
went out to the kitchen.

New-York Harbour

The lumber barge had stood in the harbour for several days and I couldn't get to shore even if it was only a mile away, because the captain wouldn't let me lower the boat. He said it leaked. There was no place to land anyway as firms owning the various storehouses and docks would not permit a boat to land on their property.

It would be very hot in the city at best, with not much to do but tramp about the streets since everybody I know was out of town for the summer. One day had gone by with fair rapidity, because I'd taken out all my bedclothes and washed them since steersmen of the barge for years back had slept on them, from their looks, with never a thought of cleanness. The second day had gone by too, because the night before bed bugs wouldn't let me sleep, even when I'd killed a hundred of them, so I was sleepy. After having taken the mattress of my cot and inspected it, ridding it of innumerable bunches of bugs, and bug's eggs, and sprinkling it with

gasoline, I let it stay out in the sun all morning.
Also I put my newspapers on the bunk that I would
put the mattress back upon, after having poured
much gasoline on it too. So in the afternoon, when
I'd made up my bunk, I was sleepy and felt sure
the bedbugs wouldn't bother me if I took a nap.
They didn't either, for that nap, though they were
back in numbers before long more indefatigably
persistent about annoying me than I was about
getting rid of them since it meant such constant
work.

The captain was a little sandy-haired Virginian,
of Scotch extraction perhaps, and though he said
he had no education, he was rather well informed,
but he didn't talk a great deal. A quiet, ironic little
man, with some adventurous romantic strain in
him since he was reading wild-west stories all
through the day, and acted quite romantically
gallant towards his wife in the evening, when we
all sat out in back of the bargecabin gazing about
us. I couldn't understand his sentiment of affection
for her. She was a narrow-shouldered, waspish person,
given to moods and sullen temperament. Generally
she didn't accompany him on his barge trips, but
this time she was doing the cooking for the three
of us, and drawing salary because of that. But she'd
refuse to serve meals on time, and if he happened
to have gone to town in a motor boat that came
along to pick him up — we both couldn't be gone
from the barge at one time — she wouldn't feed me

any dinner at all. However she wasn't cross, just crabbedly sickly perhaps, for she was as kind as could be to a little black rat-terrier bitch and her puppy that were on the barge with us. In the evenings I'd race up and down the deck having the black dog race after me, barking excitedly and snapping playfully at my heels. The puppy, a lumpy awkward ball, would do his best to follow, but he got tangled up with himself all the time, and if I should suddenly turn around and bark at him vehemently, he'd turn tail and catapult back to the captain's wife, and then look at me a little shamefacedly out of his bead-bright eyes, once he knew all was well... So I accepted the captain's wife as a woman with not a bad heart, but so long-faced, sallow, drab, and sinewy in her skininess was she that it was hard to understand his affection. Now and then she'd make a curtly humourous remark. So I concluded that beneath, her Virginia Mountain manner of silence, and almost austerity, was whimsicality of a sort to attract him.

This night had followed an eventless day, with no flairups between the captain and his misses about her not taking enough trouble with the meals, and no kick on either of their part because I didn't keep enough wood chopped.

After contemplating the statue of Liberty for a time, and reflecting on the strict limitations that there are in the concept «Liberty», I came and sat down upon a hatch cover near the Captain and his wife, a little uncomfortable because they signified nothing to me as persons, and I supposed I meant as little to them, so thought perhaps they'd rather be alone. But the ocean seemed to have cut me off from all kinds of experience I knew anything about. There was no turbulence within it tonight, only in me the consciousness of the turbulence that was a continuing quality in New-York, the habitation of turbulent masses of men and machinery.

Soon the captain got up, and walking along the side of the barge, began to see what was going by on the belly of the outgoing tide. He took the boat-hook, and would lean over the side of the barge to spear large pieces of wood to dry and use for fire-wood. Many strange things go by on the outgoing tide, intent perhaps, as I have been intent, upon merely « getting away » to taste the solitude upon the restless loneliness of ocean expanse.

« A box of whisky or I'm a sucker », the skipper said suddenly with more excitement than I'd seen him manifest before, as he pointed at a four-fifths submerged box. « The bootleggers bring whisky in to the three mile limit line and throw it over-board in boxes, to be picked up by watchers in boats, and the watchers missed that one. » He was jumping around, having found that by no straining could he touch the box with his boathook. It went by, well out of reach of us on the barge, and he talked

about it for the next three days declaring that he'd
have jumped overboard and got it, had he been
sure it was whiskey.

Still, tonight, he did not let his brooding on that
prevent his keeping a lookout for other valuable
matter that the tide might drive past.

« I've seen as many as three dead men go by in
one night ! » he commented, and I listened, not
skeptically or otherwise. The skipper was a great
liar sometimes but for all that there was no reason
to believe that he mightn't deceive one by telling
the truth occasionally, when one didn't expect it.
« Dead men », I wondered. Were they generally
bloated, did they float face down, where'd they come
from, did their folks know they were drowned,
how did their drowning come about ? Any number
of questions drifted through my mind giving iden-
tity to very impersonal dead men who go by on
the surface of an outgoing tide.

« I haven't seen any dead men go by myself, but
there are a good many of those — I suppose they're
dead men potentially — which go by every night »,
I said after a while.

The skipper looked with wary interest where I
pointed. He wasn't going to be caught napping —
not he. At first he didn't believe they were what I
told him when he asked me, but as many more
came by, and nearer the barge, he saw more dis-
tinctly. Some of them were inflated, others not,
though of course they'd all served their day.

« There's lots of them used at beaches on a holiday », he said cryptically at last.

« The unrest, the wish to go to sea attacks some of us very early in life », I suggested.

The captain's wife had heard us talking, and her curiosity got the better of her, though she wasn't so indiscreet as to ask a question in front of me. Finally however, as she was standing up, looking overboard, she saw what is was we spoke of. An enigmatic expression, partly sarcastic, partly a repressed smile, some light of recognition, showed on her face. A look was exchanged by her and the captain, and she, turning away, walked into the barge again.

It was becoming dusk and hard to distinguish whether the last animal corpse that went by was a cat, a dog, a pig, or whatnot. You can't tell what salt water will do to an animal's corpse, or can't know how long these corpses are driven back and forth by incoming and outgoing tides.

Night cupped the horizon, which dimming in the darkness was a meticulously curved arm cradling the ocean, and the opacity of distance upon unending ocean water changed into an opacity of violet gray. I stood for a time to look at the high buildings in the Wall street district of New–York, and feel the cathedral-like quality of their severity, as they pointed up in the sky towards the outcoming stars. Squares, and checkerboard designs of lights, in oblongs extending upward, appeared before me as the city lights were on, electric signboards were glimmering blue-yellow in the sky, but I could see them only as splotches of light generally, unable to discern the wordings of the lettered ones, or the illustrations of the pictorial ones. How thin, straight, and directly, skyscrapers stand against dusk of early night, when there are lights inside them. Even the ones with but few lights, stood out at first, but as the night deepened, they all became dim, vapourous, and unreal as a mirage.

It was useless standing by the side of the barge any longer, looking into the water, all black now, and not even to be seen except that my mind remembered that it was there. Besides the skipper had advised my going to bed as I'd have to get up early and chop wood before the heat of the day, as we'd probably be picked up by a towboat to-morrow afternoon, and there'd be little time to chop wood on the way down to Norfolk.

Anyway, I knew I'd have to spend at least a half hour killing bedbugs, and putting gasoline around the bed slabs, as I'd let a night go by without doing that. Gasoline is a less offensive odour to sleep with than the oily odour of bedbugs, which itch as well as smell. I detested, also, crushing a bedbug between my fingers when it was full of my own blood. So it was up to me to use gasoline in plenty.

« Your wife recognized some of those young dead men too, I noticed », I remarked to the captain as I went up the stairs of the barge cabin to my bunkroom. The captain looked a bit as though such things had not ought to be mentioned, but vouchsafed a half grin at last.

The Little Ninny

« A cat may look at a king », Goldie said, and made one realize that even if she was a rattle-brained person, or perhaps because she was so entirely pinheaded, her sentiments made a grand ideal of Tom Gladden, who had once queened her, and who now, after several years absence was revisiting the old home town. He had had many notices in the paper as a star football player since Goldie last saw him.

Goldie had changed in the intervening years too. It would be hard to conceive of her wearing a flashing purple suit, made sheath fashion with a slit to her knees, now. The change was natural of course, because it is always the younger girls in town, the ones in highschool, who giggle most exhuberantly and desire to attract all people's, particularly all men's attention, that are remarked upon. After a time the towns people get used to the fact that they've become young ladies and are pretty, or graceful, or chic, or witty, and began to wonder what kind of a marriage they'll manage to make or if they'll manage a marriage at all, and if not whether they'll teach school or drift to the city.

« Tommie certainly used to know how to make love, didn't he Marj », Goldie asked Madge Rensch, mooningly reminiscent. Madge smiled. Her dignity of carriage and hauteur were surface qualities only, because on a sleigh-ride party or a picnic she could cuddle and hug and be as free with her loving as any of them. Of course people didn't really believe that either she or Goldie would really — well, of course, they both were gay and liked a good time, but they never lost their — social position.

Strange, that in these few years Goldie had faded so amazingly. Her yellow hair was yellow as ever, and her cheeks as pink. The doll-blue stare was still in her eyes, but a sparkle that once played about her, was about her no longer. The fellows in town paid little attention to her now, not because she wouldn't fuss and cuddle as much as she ever did, but they rather felt she expected something to come of fussing and cuddling now. Goldie wanted a husband, and, not Madge — because she wanted a husband too — but some of the other girls would say that she wasn't going to be very particular either. She didn't go in much now for walking up and down the street with other girls in the town, in a new dress or hat as often as she could get one, stopping to chatter with the young men who loitered around. Oh, on vacations, when the older

men got back from college or came to visit from
various cities Goldie stilled navigated forth, but she
was an old story to the older men. Madge interested them more ; she at least had an Irish wit, and
an independent mind of a sort to carry on an
« interesting » conversation which wasn't all soft
regretful sighing for the old young days.

Then too, no fellow cares to be seen talking too
much with a girl who is willing to go around with a
grocery delivery clerk, who quite openly swaggers
around town drunk a good share of the time,
noisily talking about poker games, and the way the
various waitresses in town screw. It wasn't quite
good taste on Goldie's part to go to dances with
Tim Donaldson, even if there were so few men she
wouldn't get taken otherwise.

But when Tom Gladden struck town, he seemed
exhuberantly glad to see Goldie. « She's a little
mushhead all right, but... » he didn't quite know
what to say to justify her, since his initiation into
loving had been conducted by Goldie in the days of
their not-so-far-away past. Besides, Tom saw the
look in Goldie's eyes, knew it to be reverential
towards him, and wondered.

So he made an appointment to call on her in the
evening and then strolled off to talk about the
various football conquests of the old days when he
was captain of the town highschool team, and it
was the champion team of the state. How well he,
and the other fellows too, remembered this or that

play — a run across eighty yards of the field, a trick shift and punt, or a great tackle. At last that conversation gave out however, because Len O'Brien, and Jerry Porter, who'd been figures themselves in the town as football players, didn't care to sit around worshipping at Tom's shrine. Others than he'd have made names for themselves if they'd had a chance to go away to college. So Tom began to tell them of others things he'd done in the city — of women.

And when he left the bunch to go to dinner he remarked: « Anything doing with Goldie. She seems to have relaxed a little, doesn't she ? »

The next day Tom said nothing about Goldie, and paid little attention to her for the rest of his stay in town. When anybody mentioned Tom to Goldie a struck look came into her eyes and she hesitated, waiting for the conversation to shift without quite the ability to change the subject herself.

« Goldie's a silly little idiot », Madge commented. « If Tom had any brains what does she think she could mean to him, and did she think that news-paper notice had made a Sir Galahad out of him. I never thought though she'd have sense enough to see through Tom enough to realize she'd been heroizing a dub. »

Madge however did not know that Goldie had not realized anything about Tom, except that after years, and her idealization of him, he could ask her, casually, what he had asked.

But Goldie married Tim Donaldson, now has five children, and as to her social status the degree of her happiness, how are these things judged? Madge's husband was a hardware store owner; Gertrude's husband a barber; several other husbands were travelling salesmen, some were bank clerks, grain dealers and the conversation of them all...?

Because Tom died a year or so after Goldie married, and because she grew — not less silly perhaps — more used to real motives than to ideal in men, and in women, she manages to extract much that is sweet in remembering Tom, and in re-reading the vast sheath of letters which he once wrote to her.

Summer

There was no use. I was tired of college, and seventeen is young enough, so I could stay out a year or so. Mother herself couldn't give me any reasons for staying in college except that « it's a good idea to have a degree ».

So I looked for a job, and got one. You can always get a job if you'll ask enough places — go to the top of an office building and ask at every office till you get one. The flour business didn't mean anything in my young life but I didn't give a hurrah what job it was I had. The guts of some of these guys that employ you too! The manager of the Sawdust Flour Co had a name that fitted him properly, Mr. Bull, and he was always roaring. He had me take an examination in arithmetic to see what department he should put me into and said I had only one answer right out of ten problems. I'll bet he was a liar. I always was good in arithmetic. He thought I'd ask for more money if I knew I'd done better than the average.

Then he said to me « You'll take the salary we

give you, and work the hours we want you to, and not ask for a raise before we're ready to give it, will you? We treat our employees right in the long run but we don't want any restless employees. »

The nerve ! I was rather embarrassed by him, not afraid, but he bellowed so loudly. « Well I don't think I'll quite trust all of my career to your discrimination », I told him and grinned. I knew he liked me ; heard him say to one of the sub-execut- ives that I was a bright lad. Huh ! a bright lad, and he paid me seven dollars a week and put me into the flour testing laboratory to wash bottles under a German chemist, alongside with the half-nutty nephew of one of the rich men in the firm. It was a firm policy to start everybody at the bottom, I'd hear about me all the time.

You can take it from me they weren't going to keep me on any job like that for long. I went into Mr. Bull's office one day, and he could blurt out at me if he wanted to, I waited till he wasn't busy and asked him for a raise. When he said « You stay where you are at the salary you're getting or quit », I quit. He didn't think I would. Seven dollars a week and working under a guy named Bull in an office where everybody talks in whispers when he's around ! Me ? I guess not.

I couldn't get to Europe because that was the year that Wilson was inaugurated as President and the change of party had made steel shipping on the great lakes decrease. So when I arrived in Duluth to ship in a lake boat to Buffalo I found that there were three hundred men hanging around the docks out of work. O these lake men are hard birds. Some of them thought I looked easy and asked me for money. After the second day I didn't have any if I had been easy, and slept for three nights in box cars. One of the guys picked me up and took me around a bit and tried to help me get a job; and to tell me how to act with the rougher guys. He said I ought to go home, because he could see I'd been used to a good home.

« There's nothing in being a bum » — that stuff sounded all right. There's any number of people in all classes of society ready to sigh and moon around about the good old home stuff. I wanted life. No sticking around home and petrifying for me.

But the fellow didn't have any more money than I did and I couldn't ask men on the street for money, so I couldn't eat. Sunday morning I hadn't eaten for three days and went to the railroad track looking towards Minneapolis. Only one hundred and fifty miles. I'd walk. The first hour or so my feet were sore and I wasn't sure I wouldn't starve to death, and didn't care, but by the time I'd washed my feet in a brook I felt better and plucked up the courage to go into a farm house and ask for something to eat. The lady brushed her slimy hair out of her eyes, and sighed heavily over the child in her stomack, but her heart was in the right place even if she was slovenly. The bread was soggy as lead and the milk sour, but I was hungry.

That night I stayed at a fine farm house where they believed me when I said I was walking to Minneapolis on a bet and mustn't spend any money on the way. « These boys », the lady said after I told her a long tale. That farmer was a deacon in the village church up the road, and though I don't care for church people as a home environment, I did like the food they served me, and the fact that they offered me a bed to sleep in. I didn't take that though, because like a damn fool I'd lied more than was necessary and had said that the bet stipulated that I was not to sleep in a bed on the way. So they gave me blankets and I slept in the hayloft.

After four days of that kind of thing I reached home, just after supper, and mother gave me a bowl of strawberries and cream. She said she thought that I'd be back home about this time. The dickens, I would have got to Europe if it hadn't been for Wilson and there not being any steel shipping on the great lakes.

Home was rather nice for a day or so but good lord, my brothers and sisters got on my nerves. George and Bill had done just as many rattlebrained things as ever I did; they needn't spend so much time kidding me. Anyway mother began to talk about planting a garden and having me take care

of it through the summer. She's such a romantic
old woman. Plant a garden! Hadn't I seen George
and Bill let every garden we ever had get so full of
weeds that the family cow would get hay fever
trying to browse in them?

So I decided I'd go back to the old town in South
Dakota and take in the harvest. And what if I did
only weigh a hundred pounds. I could shock grain.
Bill and George thought they were the only people
in the world with a little muscle to hear them talk.
They gave me a belly ache. Home and family life!

You can damn well know I wasn't going to
stick around home and have to listen to the whole
family talk about what I did do, and what I didn't
do, every time I came to a meal. What did any of
them ever do to be able to talk about me? I never
asked any of them what they did when they came
in late at night, or mentioned it at the table if I saw
Bill with a dizzy blond.

Mother decided at last I might sell the house we
owned back there and gave me ten dollars for railroad fare, saying I wouldn't starve with so many
friends in that town surely.

The harvest! Why say, every freight car that went
through Merivale had several hundred men on top
of and under it, and not any of them would stay on
a job for more than a day or so. Some of them were
college students being hoboes for the summer
months. The harvest was all right. I worked for a
day or so now and then stacking hay, or shocking-

barley, but with the Chatauqua lake only four
miles from town and all the best looking girls from
four states staying in the cottages around it, it's
not to be supposed — there's something in life
besides working anyway. I didn't need money.

You should have seen Lenore Thomas — some
peach — and when I'd left town three years before
she hadn't known how to keep her face clean she
was so small. The way a flock of homely kid girls
had sprouted into a bunch of snappy flappers!
I tell you this, it's the small towns where the good
looking girls are, and they're liveliest too. In the
city only a few of the girls fuss and love but out in
South Dakota they all love. All the traveling men
that come through Merivale will tell you about the
dreams there are who'll go almost all the way when
it comes to loving, and some of them go all the way.

But Lenore wasn't that kind. No, she was a nice
girl. The only girl in town with her hair bobbed
and her hair was dark brown red. She had a nose
that tilted up a bit, a ruddy skin, and just a few
freckles, and eyes with twinkling spots in them. I
liked her very much, but Tennessee was her fellow
and he was a friend of mine, and Carl liked her
too and he was a friend of mine, so that if she ditch-
ed Tennessee I'd have to let Carl have her because
he was going to stay in town. She was jaunty and
peppy. I liked the way she cussed out her father and
mother, telling them to « go to hell ». She was peppy,
and they were whining sorts, and both pinheaded

old people. Her mother didn't want her to dance because she'd been operated on for appendicitis just a month ago, but she could tell her mother where to head in at. With a dance on at the hotel every night she couldn't sit around and twiddle her fingers all the time.

I was going down the street one day and saw Lenore tripping my way; there was style, real class to the way she walked; I had on overalls and a dirty shirt as I'd been looking for a job shocking for a day or so to have spending money.

« Hello, Bennie! » she hailed me. « You look just like a hobo. » « That's what I am », I answered her, and had to laugh because I heard some fellows who'd come in on the freight cars saying that people thought a man was a hobo simply because he'd take a free vacation now and then, and they were petulant about it.

Dawgone it, I liked Lenore. She liked me too, but there were Tennessee and Carl, and she liked them too. Well I liked Helen Chatford too ; and Genevieve Manners; and Neva Moss, and Leila Fitzgerald. There were so many pretty girls in town. Helen wasn't pretty but she could follow every movement of your body when she danced with you, and had read more than most girls in town. Her aunt taught in the city and she talked about going to Vassar, or Wells, or Smith. Yes, yes. Lots of them in town, fellows and girls too, talk and decide to go to Byrn Mawr, or Harvard, or Yale, or perhaps more exclusive and smaller schools. But they usually decide to sell shirts at one of the stores in town or teach school after going to the normal ; or maybe marry a farmer or a travelling salesmen. It's too bad there's not more men around for the older girls, as good looking as they are, but any fellow with get–up to him goes away from the old town before he's fixed for marrying.

Tennessee and Carl and I'd go out with girls who lived on the other side of the lake sometimes ; not much class to them, but Tennessee thought maybe there'd be something doing. But there wasn't. None of us got what we wanted. You could fuss your damned head off, and they'd go so far and no further, and then because they'd want to see you again, say that maybe they'd come across another night. Maybe one of them came across for Tennessee because he had the « social disease » when I left town, but he wouldn't say where'd he got it. Carl was a little afraid. I don't think he really tried to start anything with any of the girls. He was too well brought up.

The Chautauqua season was over and there wasn't so much dancing, or so many girls in crowds anymore, so I decided I'd do about a month of solid harvesting so as to have a pile of money when I got back to the city. I waited till Monday though before looking for a job, and in waiting, on Saturday night, went to a dance at the town dancehall. Then I danced with Lily Jameson, and my Lord, how she

climbed when she danced, and she was one of the
most careful girls that ever lived three years ago.
When Tom Gladden threw her over, and she had to
take to playing the piano in the moving picture
theatre for a living she must have decided there
wasn't any use in being too careful. I thought it
strange that she didn't go the city, with a mind
like hers, and ability to play as she had. She might
go on the stage. There was something electric about
her personality, and exhuberantly cleanly voluptuous about her slimness. But she said she didn't
have enough money to take a chance on the city.

After the dance I struck down the road from
Merivale to Lansing, a smaller town ten miles away,
where an uncle of mine lived. There were woods on
both sides of the road and no moon was out. I
could hear cracklings in the woods, and stumbled
along on the rough road; startled once by the
hooting of an owl. I was just enough afraid of the
dark to insist to myself that I must walk right on,
and the little fear gave a zest to walking. There is
freedom in the night cool air, and sometimes in
lapses where fields lay between sections of woods,
odours of alfalfa hay, or clover, came to me.

I reached Lansing finally, and woke my uncle
who lived in a house all alone. He came to the
door, glad that I was there if it was three o'clock in
the morning. I don't think he had been asleep.
Something was the matter with his mind. He told
me about voices he'd been hearing, people whisper–

ing in his ear all the time. As I came into the house, there was no light, I touched him, and felt his thin body through his nightshirt, and he clung to me, shivering, not with cold because it was a warm night, but with fear. I wished I could help him, get him away from this lonely tiny village, and living in solitude in this big house that had once been the home of a big family, now all gone away from him.

But I couldn't think my way through about him. Perhaps he would die and that would solve his problem. He told me that one night the week before he'd been chased by a woman who'd come to him and wanted him to stop praying and come and sleep with her. It angered him because the owner of the little grocery store down the one street in the village said that he had imagined all that. « I know I see people that other people don't see, but they are real people. They are after me », he said.

There wasn't any use of my brooding over his situation. I had no money. The next day I waited around the village poolhall until farmers came into town, and finally picked up with one who took me out in the country with him to feed shocks to the threshing machine. He was a erect, blocky-faced German, and I judged that I'd get good food at his place, and kindlier treatment than from some farmers I'd worked for, who thought of nothing but getting a long days work out of their men and horses...

Because summer was almost over, because my

uncle's condition made me brood, and because I'd
tired of being out night. after night dancing and
making love to the girls, I felt reflective and sad as
I rode out with Mr. Martin to his farm. I was tired
inside myself, wondering whether life really matters,
what I should do after I returned to the city, and I
was not wanting to return to the city.

Here was the country with a clean sky above it,
and clean fields stretching out around me. I
remembered how years before in this part of the
country I could pick wild strawberries and flowers
along the field fences, and get up now and then to
look across the grainfields over which sunlight
poured bubbling yellow; and the wind between
the stalks of grain had made the ripening fields
seem to breath and pulsate with the flux of life
expanding.

« You're a slight lad », Mr. Martin said. « I'll
have to let you drive my black team and bring
hayrack's of hay to the stack I guess. You'd break
in two handling a fork if you had to keep up with
the older men. »

He could do what he wished. At that moment I
had no desires regarding my future, immediate,
or far away. If I couldn't stand the work he could
get rid of me.

When we got to his farm he introduced me to
his wife and that surprised me a trifle because
most farmers just grunt about having a new man,
to help them. Mrs. Martin surprised me too, because

she was beautiful in a fragile, porcelain way, with peach red cheeks, and tired large eyes, the violet of which was intensified by the fine blue skin about them. Plainly she was gentile. I was surprised too when after supper she said I could have a bath if I wished and took me to a bath room with a big tub and hot and cold water faucets. Farms in South Dakota don't have such equipment generally. I thought probably Mr. Martin was a college bred farmer, but found out later that he wasn't. They were simple farmer folk with some strain of refinement in them that was beyond mere kindheartedness.

In the morning John Martin woke me at six and a little later we had breakfast, but did not go to work until seven. « Seven till twelve, and half past one till six unless later is absolutely necessary to save a crop is my rule », Mr. Martin said, and I knew I'd struck a soft job as farm jobs go.

When we had gone to the stable and hitched the horses to the hayracks out come the two Martin girls, Sadie and Nellie, and their younger brother and sister, and all clambered into the wagon.

« It's making hay for me, or working in the field, everytime before housework », Sadie comment-ed. The fact that they were going to work along-side me rather bothered me because I looked at both her and Mabel and concluded that they were huskier than I was. It wasn't quite suitable that they should be able to work harder than I.

The first day we were to stack the remainder of the year's last cutting of hay which had lain on the field for almost a week, and would be lost entirely if it should rain. I was driving a jumpy pair of shiny black horses, blockily built but neat lined, with well shaped heads and intelligent eyes. This was the first time I had ever driven a team of horses to have to back up to a stack and get into position all alone, and I was ill at ease; not because of timidity regarding the horses but because I felt I must be more awkward about driving them than the horses were about being driven.

The two girls went with me in the rack when we got to the hayfield, to pick up hay, while Mr. Martin and his son John worked around the stack, building up the hay. The girls had their sleeves rolled up so that I could see the upper portion of their arms; my sleeves were also rolled up, and I was much at a disadvantage in arm diameter and believed that they must be looking me over with some disdain. It didn't disturb me that Nellie had disdain for me because she was rather heavy faced with no sparkle of charm about her; but Sadie, in spite of quiet manner, had a resilient buoyancy of body and carriage that made me want to touch her, and to have her like me.

I knew there was nothing for me to be but a farmer; to have many beautiful horses, a few well-kept hogs, some jersey cattle, chickens, and just

a few golden pheasants and peacocks to strut
around my place. I began to plan the model kind
of farm I'd have ultimately, and didn't know but
I'd include Sadie in the other model equipment.
But diffidence kept me from being able to talk
much to her. After we fell to working though we
began to talk and she told me about the country
school she went to, and the books she read, and
about taking music lessons, and what she wanted
to do after she was through school.

At ten o'clock Mrs. Martin brought a lunch for
us all out to the field and we ceased work for half
an hour; at twelve we went in for dinner, returning
to work at one thirty; at four we had another
lunch; and at shortly after six were sitting around
the back of the house waiting to be called for
supper. At eight we all were sitting in the parlour
and I was telling John Martin about the city, and
college, and he was telling me about his collection
of stamps, and his intentions of going to an agricultural college, and of a correspondence course
in shorthand he was taking. Sadie played the piano,
and finally began to sing songs from a school
songbook. I had to join in then, and soon was
singing lustily « A Spanish Cavalier » and « Over
the Bounding Main ».

When I went to bed I lay for a time thinking
about the kind of farm I would have some day.
This was the kind of life to lead. Simple and clean
and healthy, with no grindling hard work either,

not when you manage well. A feeling of clarity,
and consummate realization was in me ; a knowledge of space and stretches of country fields about
me with a sky not smokeridden overhead. But I
didn't finish the story about my future farm
because sleep overtook me.

However after five days working there I liked
the Martins all very well but knew this kind of
life wasn't for me ; Saturday afternoons, and
some weekday afternoons in a slack season
going in to the village to shop and loiter about the
streets for an hour or so; on Sunday mornings
driving to church; on Sunday afternoons going
swimming or picnicing at a lake in summertimes
and calling on friends in the wintertime. I'd get
tired of the monotony of such a routine. My nature
was not that tranquil. I was rather wishing to be
back in the city because in my memory was the
illusion of colour and activity and more sensitive
understanding of my desires there, though when I'd
reflect I knew that once in the city I'd find it
grinding and tiresome too, permitting me too many
long hours that I didn't know what to do with.

The third night when I'd gone to bed I was torn
with desire ; imagined that I had a girl with me ;
not Sadie — she occurred to my mind but she did
not appeal sufficiently to my romantic fancy; seemed not rare enough, not beautiful or sufficiently
hard to attain. But I was quite sick with the disgust
of unappeased desire. It was entirely stupid and

wrong that I didn't have some girl with me. There was some impalpable barrier forever up restraining and oppressing my impulses. I must break down the barrier; smash through conventions and training and not have this hunger tormenting me. I must get back to the city soon and go to Dreamland dance hall when I got there, to pick up some girl that one did not need to be pretending with constantly. I'd have to take a chance on infection; couldn't go on like this forever. Of course I had an uncomfortable dream that night when I did finally go to sleep. The next two nights I wasn't disturbed much but slept easily and soundly.

On Tuesday, after I'd been with Mr. Martin for six days, I told him I'd have to leave and get back to the city. « Getting homesick are you laddie. I've noticed you've been brooding the last day or so, he commented. Well I won't try to keep you though I need a man for a few days more. » He paid me twenty dollars and I went to town Wednesday morning with Mrs. Martin who was driving in for groceries. I felt rather guilty for not staying to see Mr. Martin through stacking his grain, but could not quell the desire to be off that raged within me. All of Tuesday I'd lifted every forkfull of grain shock with a toxin of distaste and rage at the necessity of doing such monotonous work in my mind and heart.

I went to see my uncle as soon as I got in town and told him that I was going back to the city that night. He wanted me to stay with him a few days, assuring me that he'd buy extra good food and take care of me well. Guiltily I told him that it was necessary that I go back to the city at once; and I reasoned to myself that feeling guilty was foolish because my staying a few days would not help uncle's situation of loneliness and senile-minded terrified imaginings. I could not understand, and would not accept the need of going on with life in such situations as his. The solution was somebody else's than mine.

So at five o'clock I boarded the train that was to take me back to Minneapolis. Such a train! full of families who had their lunches spread out on their laps or spread all over the seat next to them; and several small babies whimpering and crying; and children with sticky hands and messy faces, running up and down the aisles eternally to get a drink of water or to go to the toilet room. I was savagely uncommunicative to anybody who tried to start a conversation with me; contemptuous of every human being I could see around me.

Burning inside with various disgusts I listened detestingly to the hearty insistent laughter and vulgar stories of three travelling salesmen who were sitting in the four seats at the end of the car.

Fat oily specimens of fatuous haberdasher idealists they seemed to me. When they asked me if I wanted to join a foursome of poker I embarrassedly declined, not wanting them to think me snobbish, feeling a desire to escape myself for a moment, to have them like me, still retaining within myself an intense distaste for them. But my intelligence was telling me that such sullen brooding as that of my present mood was foolishness.

After a time I fell asleep, curled across the seat, and did not awake till seven o'clock in the morning. My neck was a trifle stiff at first, the muscles on the side of my face I had slept on were asleep and the skin blotchy; my eyes were sticky, and a gluey taste was in my mouth. Rubbing my hand across my eyes a sensation of unreality went through me; everything in the world seemed hazy, sticky, not worth the poignancy of despair.

The train came into the Union station at Minneapolis and I dismounted, took a streetcar, and was home at eight o'clock. Mother kissed me saying « Well, you're back, are you » and went on about getting breakfast. She was too used to having her youngsters come and go without announcement.

I had a bowl of oatmeal, with toast and coffee, and while I was eating my brothers and sisters came in gradually and began to ask me about people they knew back in Merivale, and about the amount of money I'd made. In talking I of course became exhuberant, saying how wonderful it was at Chatauqua lake, and how well all the girls back in the old town were dressing now — better than in Minneapolis — how well they danced the new dances. I was feeling quite cheerful again.

After breakfast I walked across the bridge to see the city streets of Minneapolis again, and feel city traffic about me. The day was hot; the tar on the creosote pavement blocks melted so that in crossing the street one's feet stuck a bit ; sultriness and stuffy odours were in the air.

« What'd I come back to the city for so soon », I asked myself, and was quite disgusted that I hadn't stayed out in South Dakota to take in the corn husking season.

Snow

The prairies of North Dakota lay a foot under snow, so that everywhere the eyes could see was gray whiteness, for the snow having been on the ground for some weeks was dirtied with dust that the wind had thrown upon it. In gullies, and in various spots where the eddies of gale had blown it, snow rested in heaps six to ten feet deep. The sun was out shining over all this whiteness so that a dazzle was in the air, and a clarity that was rather irksome, because in walking along one felt its sting in the eyes, and had to stumble somewhat in walking.

Clara and Christabel Herne had both given up their positions as school teachers in country schools out from Beach, and had come to spend a few days with their brother Sam, before going out to live in their shack on a claim they'd taken a few months before.

All of the Herne's were queer people; not merely stupid, but lackadaisical, and seemingly unaware one minute what they had done the moment before.

Clara and Christabel were both near forty, huddling little old maids who would sit and plan indecisive plans for getting their claim lands into shape to farm. It appearently did not occur to them that to say that you will do such and such, does not do away with the problems that obstruct the way to accomplishment. Sam was a heavy, broodingly apathetic sort of a man. A stigma of almost unbelievable helplessness and incompetency was upon them all.

On Thursday Sam drove around to his house with his team of horses and a sleigh, and Clara and Christabel helped Sam and his wife put blankets, pillows, flour, bacon, bread, and other food supplies into the back of the sleigh. When they thought that there was enough supplies to feed Clara and Christabel for two weeks out in their shack, the two girls got into the sleigh with Sam, and off they all drove, fifteen miles across the snow.

Upon arriving, as it was about four o'clock in the afternoon and beginning to get dusk, Sam was in a hurry to start back home as driving over the little settled country would be hard if he waited till dark. So he hastily dumped out all of the supplies that were in the sleigh and said goodbye. After he had driven away the women went into the shack and stood looking around them for a minute or so, indecisive about what to start to do, to get the shack in order, and settle down to a routine of living.

« I guess we'd better light a fire, hadn't we Christabel », Clara volunteered.

There was wood in the fireplace, and two sacks of
coal amongst the supplies which they had brought
with them, but on searching they found not one match.
So they stood for a time looking at each other.

« Well, I do believe we didn't bring any matches », Christabel said. The two stood and looked
helpless. It did not occur to either of them to run
out and holloa after Sam; it did not flash into
their minds what a predicament they were in.
Their minds did not work that way.

« Why, we may freeze to death if we don't have
a fire », Clara asserted after standing dazedly for a
time, not dazed with fright; only with the abstracted helplessness that was typical of them both.

When it did occur to Christabel to go out and
look across the snow neither of them could see
Sam's sleighwagon any longer. Even if he were not
far away it was too dusk for them to see him now;
and they could not run after him because they
would readily have been lost in all that prairie
expanse of snow in the dark. But it did not occur
to either of them to run after him, and had they
started walking in the direction that he had gone
they would have gone absent-mindedly, having
lapsing moments of forgetfulness of their intention
to try and reach town again.

That night they slept close to each other, huddled
up in the blankets which they had, that were suffic-

ient to keep them from freezing to death. The morning after was a clear day and they could now have readily followed the tracks of Sam's sleigh back to town, and perhaps not have had to walk all of the fifteen miles, since some farmer might have picked them up when they reached a main road eight miles from town into which many little-used roads ran.

However they did not start to walk back to town. They puttered around the house saying to each other « If we work getting things into shape the exercise will keep us warm. » « Perhaps Sam will remember that we haven't any matches and come to bring us some today. »

And they knew, or should have known, that Sam was not given to remembering much of anything.

Again and again they searched every box of supplies they had hoping to find some matches. Their figures seemed more weazened and drawn up into knots than ever.

Then the wind began to blow a gale ; the snow began to fall, and was at last whirling around their shack in terrific currents so that they couldn't be sure it wouldn't blow away. The snow was a cutting, sleet hard snow, one could tell by the rattle of it against the window pane of the shack.

« You know, dear, we should have tried to walk back to town while it was clear », Clara commented, as always realizing the proper action long after an ordinary person would have realized it.

It blizzarded for three days, so that the snow was screwed up into great heaps all over the plain, with not a path or road to be seen in any direction.

Ten days after he had brought his sisters to their shack, and after it had been calm for an entire week it occurred to Sam that he'd better drive out and see them, bringing them some more supplies. « I didn't give them any too much coal to last them you know », he told his wife.

But Sam's journey was useless. When he came to the shack he found his sisters bound up in blankets, cuddled to each other, frozen quite dead.

The Futility of Energy

A friend of Raymond's said of him that he did not paint because he was disillusioned ; knew art to be a profession, and its market to be commercialized ; knew that men are « great » in their day only because we lack perspective ; and realized that old masters need not be deified, as however individual their response to life may have been and their skill to record it in cold esthetic terms with a respectable degree of discernment, they still come well within the scope of comprehension of any person with sentiency, intellect, and audacity in experience. There needs to be mystery for there to be revererence. Of course Raymond did not go in for emotional luminousness and exaltations, but believed that much fervour about spirituality, nobility and genius has simple sensuous and religiously desiring sources. He, as have others, tired of faiths, gods, and moralities clung to because of frustrated human yearnings, and wished to accept temporal existence temporally, and real experience rationally.

Neither the friend nor Raymond, however, realized that it is not disillusionment to stop at disill-
usion — too emotional that — so long as there be
energy extant and one lives wishing in some way
to express that energy in a manner satisfying to
one's intelligence... They possibly knew too much
of modern art, what has been done and can't be
done again by people of pride, even if they did not
seem to realize that twenty centuries before the
twentieth century philosophers played cynically
with doctrines of futility, inactive apathies — sens-
sitive people feel as well as think of the oppressive
ignorance and insentiency of the public and of
even highly enlightened beings about them. Naturally in a world where all is profession, commerce,
marketing, and attempt to build a foundation of
standard moralities and sentimentalities to protect
life-frightened people from cosmic terror, a man
of exploring sincerity finds himself obliterated
from the major consciousness by the fact that
he is calmy ignored ; and if he stops there —
insufficiently detached — a trifle romantic and
sentimental yet about life to indulge in despair
because his expectancies are revolted — eternally
adolescent then — human intelligence is always
immature — then he never realizes that he can
obliterate the obtuse public and its aggressively
assertively obtuse individuals who combat him,
by ignoring it and them also for their acclaims or
disdains. It isn't cold contempt or rebellion, or de-

fiance that man needs; it is only the realization that
nobody else cares if he does not care to express
himself, and that finally inaction, and tired undoing
skepticism becomes the expression of himself. Well
— if he would only put the force of his tired convictions back of t ese qualities he might create
works of power — and notwithstanding general
stupidities, find audience, for if there is one thing
that many people feel, it is a sense of futility.

Raymond was a young man with lovely qualities.
There was nothing anyone could say to him that
he would not understand — no assertive dogma
narrowness, or moral prejudices within him; not
too much will either. Across his sensitive oval face
his broodingly spiritual eyes gave the impression
at once, to who could see, of kind wise intuitions.
His bitterness was not aimed at people, or at things,
or even at life, unless to suffer inside oneself is
directing bitterness at life. A high forehead, a high
acquiline nose of fragile bony structure, a sweet
straight mouth that intellect and fine disdain kept
from drooping in an over-melancholy manner, and
a chin ovaled subtly with a graciously swooping
downcurve from his ears — a soft straight line from
his lips — made his face contemplative and gentle.
Such people as he was apt to be with — artists
mostly — were always fond of or adoring towards
him. Men often liked to pat his arm, put their arms
about him in an affectionate embrace, and some of
them liked to kiss him. He permitted this out of

kindly lassitude, too sophisticated and aware that
nature either makes some people different than
others -- or that imagination does — to let them
know that their kisses were distasteful to him, if
all of them were so.

« What work do you do ? » a « now who can this
notable person be » inquisitive lady asked him one
night.

« That's no question to ask Raymond, feeling
as he does », someone spoke for him and Raymond
added :

« I almost blush every time the question is asked
me. There should always be a person around to
tell what other persons around do or do not do,
to save them the embarrassment of talking about
themselves. »

There are people who are able to sense the
significance of almost any possible human experience, even as children; simply organisms keyed
higher — and lower — than usual. They are organs
of gradated tone and life plays upon them what
symphony it will, granting them some leeway as
conductors in the matter of choice if they will to
make decisions, and believe in selection. Raymond
was such an organism. At nineteen, in France, he
comprehended life — say subconciously — better
than many « artists » are ever able to.

It may be true that there is nothing new in the
world, or nothing old, since each temperment per-
ceives personally — (that can be contradicted) —

but Raymond came at a time when it appeared that every type of emotional expression in art has been too well expressed to need expression again. A point that, since even scientific zeal and intellectual detachment have emotion as a motivating force. At any rate Raymond was sufficiently ironical and « detached » never to indulge in things mystical, romantic, or sentimentally sentimental — which of course even an ideal of abstract beauty or of understanding becomes upon becoming a convention, but neverfear, so long as there are human minds, the ideal won't become a convention in its purity, since distortion and misapprehension are attained with much great facility.

Rightly or wrongly, Raymond believed that art must be reflective, discerning ; must create new experience, explore, and re-interpret in a manner that withstands the sternest intellectual diagnosis, but with a re-interpretation that is simply more discerning recordation rather than a preachment. Form against form, colour against colour, to make a form and colour music with more than decorative impact, and back of these a mature realization of life's signification, was what he sought to express. To have accepted reality, mortality, pain, obscenity, tedium — to the extent of being a little incapable of knowing which is which in the routine chaos of experience — and still to believe in exploration... a picture that Raymond painted was given much newspaper attention which praised it with ornate

17

stupidities or scoffed at it because it did not have
qualities that he deliberately wanted it not to have.
But newspapers are edited by people who have
learned what art is, they've seen examples of it —
Raymond's picture ? — well, there are points in
human psychology that newspapers seem to fail
either to understand or to be interested in. In spite
of the fact that newspaper men know that all men
like publicity whether they protest they do or not,
Raymond winced subjectively because of notice
that was to him insolent, cheap, flippant, blunder-
ingly intrusive, and perhaps malicious for there
seemed no reason that he alone should be made a
target for over-attention.

Of course he was among the first of the moderns,
in an age caught up in a swirl of « modern art »,
poetry, painting, music, dancing. Purportedly the
movement signified a breakaway from set in dogmas
of the art world, but naturally mortals could not
stand so taut a strain as that. The moon, love, chast-
ity, purity, all of which had ceased to be spoken of
in contemporary print for a period, leaped towards
ecstatic acclaim again. Ladies who had lived with
ten men wrote verses on faithfulness ; men who
didn't know how to carry on a conversation with a
pure chaste woman, and who found her tiresome,
began to write as poets have always written about
virtues that we are supposed to exalt and disdain
to possess. Young manly ladies, and girlish boys,
too shy and well brought up to actually mean what

they said, said all sorts of things that caused ladies
to begin to dote on hearing their poetry read at
teas. The porcelain crockery and lillies were left
alone — except in France — because Chinese jade,
faint shadows, delicate reminiscence, and flirtation
with the macabre in one school, and perspiring
brothermankind, prairie yodels, industrial atmosphere, and real roughstuff, in the other school,
seemed more fitting subject matter for modern
verse. Tiredly cultured adolescents drooped over
teacups, in verses at least, and became morbidly
metaphysical ; several English and American
ladies and gentleman became rhapsodically Greek
and amorous ; self-conscious young men departed
from other continents than their native one, and,
newly rich to art's necessity and culture, scolded
the world, and particularly their country for being
as damn dumb and insensitive as it always has
been. Importation of ideas, information, sermons
on religious-to-life realisms, forced emotional ladies
to editing magazines that articles and art might be
advertised — the plane became astral with art
rather than with theosophy. Discussion about form
was rife ; colour and rhythm theories were evolved
and pursred to their ultimate nothingnesses; sym-
phonic poems were orchestrated about melancholy
moods because aging dilletante lovers feminisced
when faint music played ; sentimental mercenary
egotists, soft and sighingly gentle after years of
poverty and sex repressions, indulged in philo-

sophical whimsicalities about garden vegetables;
the years passed with poets turned critics, wending
a literary way searching for « something more
subtly beautiful and refined » — while outside
things were about as crude, vulgar, and all too
real, as ever. Never did ague make men to quiver as
over-sensitivity caused highly organized completely sensitized poets and poetesses to tremble and
sweat. Innumerable people learned the colour and
cadence of words, and the force that a literary
connotation gives them; they could make words
fly, swoop, sweep, sink, float — if words were made
of substance there would have been no need for
airplanes, or oceangoing vessels. Continents of
people could have been transported where they
wished by words. As to discernment ? — What has
that to do with poetry ? A romantic nature can
brood over an image made to be an image —
romantic natures do not analyse. ...Numberless
accusations were made by numberless critics who
perhaps themselves wrote poetry that numberless
other poets had not the slightest conception of
what poetry is, was, or might be.

Though not visually discernable many there
were fainting with sensitivity, swooning with
beauty, frozen to pallorous icebergs of ecstacy
that like « diamonds cut themselves by their own
dust to fragilely imagined images. »

The conditions in the domain of painting were
not so exaggerated, since some preparation is

necessary to get paint upon canvass, and both
paint and canvass cost money, but there too, new
schools sprung up in defiance to defend « sanity ».
The new schools were mainly of intellectual cold-
ness, scientific, searching to chart human experience along newer lines than the rediscovered
principles of Greek design. Daring souls disdained
the Greeks, acclaimed the Chinese, and torrented
on to applaud primitive and negro art, while straining for the enigmatical contemplative profundity
of Eastern art. In a search for form some modern
artists, insistent upon form, the absolute, and still
insistently rational, failed to reflect that they were
going headon into mysticism in insisting upon any
absolute. Before five years had passed any number
of sculptors and painters, of Jewish extraction
generally, had managed to twist cold rationality
and scientific zeal for form to the end that « substance does not matter ; all is spirit », or « we are
looking for the soul of things. » To which statements others would reply « A thing is what it is. »

Naturally ironic intellectuals became playful over
all this, tired of unperceptive emotional intensity.
Into their vocabulary came phrases such as « the
accident of form » as they proclaimed their disbe-
lief in anything but the trivial while making a not
un-heavy faith out of their faith in naughty
nihilism.

Raymond, having surveyed the scene for several
years had seen old colleagues go on to recognition

that established them economically. In disgust of
the professionalism in the art world he had gone to
America to live, and after a four year period of a
world war, spent his years half and half in France
and America. Before this time he had ceased to
find it amusing to himself to attempt the creation
of accidents of form with esthetic significence,
because he knew that a spot in the street, or a splotch
on a window pane, the shape of a cloud, could as
well achieve the accidentally esthetic as he could
by firing lead bullets through a pane of glass for
the design the splinters made. It was just as useless
to stand away from his canvass and throw paint at
it, since the novelty was by for him, for his admir-
ers, and paint is expensive. He was not an ordinarily stupid person, not a trifler by disposition,
but one more specialized, organized and sensitized,
so that he was incapable of asserting loudly any
self–protective dogmas. In him was an emotional
dependency that wished for minds about him that
could understand what he might think, feel, and
try to paint. He needed contempt that was colder
than that of his nature, so that irony instead of
turning upon his inside being might turn upon the
outside world and not leave the wound of apathy
upon his sensibilities. However quick one's wit, and
broad one's comprehension, one can't disbelieve
in one's own value and still create, and the spectacle of inane contemporary humanity and intellectuals need not shut of the fact that there is

understanding — and that if it were general neither art nor religion would be necessary.

On a Saturday night « evening » at Dawsons, who was a patron of the arts, agnostically, Raymond drifted in at about twelve o'clock, and began to tell of the new negro club where a jazzy negress met you at the door and extracted ten dollars from you, before conducting you to the club rooms, where you could dance, gamble, listen to jazz, or chatter. Between interest in geometric constructions, life informally lived, and entertainment spontaneously happened upon, Raymond was managing to convince himself that in pursuing the casual and accidental he was being natural, and not at all tainted with arty art mannerisms.

Blair Howland had been telling some of her filthiest comic stories, wonderfully vulgar, profane, and Rabelaisian as she — a wild horse sort of a girl — could be upon inspired occasions when she had an audience which drew her out. Quite a bit soft and sentimental beneath her arrogance, and majestic gesturings, but the crust was defiant, contemptuously hardboiled and outspoken.

« For Christ's sake, don't ask me to tell any more stories », she had just asserted. « Do I get paid for amusing you people; do I want to amuse you? I tell these things because I'm bored stiff and like to have things pass off easily... and you needn't tell me I'm beautiful, or clever — I don't give a Christer's damn — some of the rest of you hop to it and entertain me for a while to prove that your admiration's worth angling for. »

« But, Blair, you're too rough, and also too exclusive. »

« Rough ? — yes, that's Blair. She will act like a bloody whore and be the chastest woman in the country, when with her figure she could have been riding in a limousine for these last ten years. »

« Huh, me ? Nope, I'm not made that way. I'm the kind of woman that good men fall in love with while they remain true to their wives, and talk about my big soul. Even prizefighters let me interview them — and they usually won't let women within a mile of their training quarters. »

« O, Blair, do tell again so Raymond can hear about the interview you had with Jack Dempsey. »

« O — well — O no, dearie — I've told that three times already, and my illustrative gestures are getting mechanical. »

« You must write up your life, Blair; it's been so remarkable — all the muck of obscene experience before you were half grown so that you knew how to be obscenely comic very young. »

« Write it ? — Mebbe. That takes energy, and hope — and who'd publish the results — think of the scandal — besides things written sound different than things said, and the typewriter doesn't draw me out. »

« That's right », Raymond broke in on the comments filtering through the cigarette smokish

atmosphere. « Don't you become serious about
literature, Blair, even humourous literature. That'd
spoil a good comedian. »

« You would say that Raymond, you just would.
Christ in a blossoming garden you'd be a nice boy
if you hadn't become artistic too young — why
don't you let yourself go someday and be as
sentimental as you actually are? » Blair said.

« And you? »

« Righto, Raymond, you and I are on to each
other. Me with my haughty gestures. — »

« Blair, are you going to make love to Raymond? » some one broke in.

« It would have to be me starting a thing of that
sort. He doesn't believe in romance. I say to think
you feel an emotion and make the most of it. »

« But you rush the fence too hard and frighten
all timid response away. »

« Who wants timid response. I want 'em wild
and rough. »

« Tuts my dear — and you devoting your life
and salary to supporting down and outers. »

« I know. I'm always taking care of somebody, or
protecting somebody, and I'm tired of it. Wish someone would come along and protect me for a while;
the travail of competence and ability is ghastly. »

« I'll protect you, Blair » Raymond said, and
patted her arm, « this evening anyway. Careful
now people; don't any of you mistreat this child «
he shook his finger at the others in the room, all of

them a bit swirling minded with wine and whiskey.
A little later, after a drink or so as he sat on the
arm of Blair's chair with his arm resting across
her shoulders, he leaned over and kissed her on
the neck.

« What is that Raymond — passion, protection,
or simply lust? » Blair asked.

« Surely you're not asking for an analysis of
impulse? » he answered.

« No » she said, disinterestedly « let it pass as a
moment's diversion. I don't suppose you'd dare
permit yourself to be interested — might hurt you
later on to lose — ah well, there you are », and she
got up from her chair, stroked him on the chin and
strolled away. « I'm going home. Need sleep; not
for beauty but because my job requires energy —
no, you stay right here, Raymond. I'm used to
darker and stormier nights than this, or than you
are, and I'm not up to protecting you tonight. »
A few minutes later she strode out. Soon the rest
of the party began to depart. When most of them
were gone Raymond told Dawson he'd nap till
morning on a lounge if it was all right, since it
was five o'clock ; whereupon he slumped to a couch
and tumbled into a doze.

At eight in the morning he was up, washed,
standing by the window, looking from the apartment window down at the city streets.

« When are you going to start painting again ? »
Dawson asked, coming up to him.

« No, no, don't. I hate painting. »

« What don't you hate, or what do you want to do ? »

« Only that. I wouldn't hate it so much if I didn't want so much to paint. »

« Don't you believe in what you have to paint? »

« But who cares whether I do or not? What's the use ? No, don't talk to me about it — it's all a game. »

For a moment as he spoke there seemed to be intensity in his voice, but in a second he shrugged his shoulders and his expression became apathetic. As he went out of the apartment door to go to a coffee house for breakfast the comment he made did not sound ironic at all, as he meant it to. It simply sounded despondent with precocious adolescent cynicism.

Momentary Essays

SKYSCRAPERS

Not that youth has any particular value in itself, but because energy needs an impulse 'behind it, and it is best that that impulse should possess exhuberance, it is well not to overstress the idea of duty since each individual desires for himself some enjoyable reason for existence. If it were possible that human intelligence become sufficiently cold and detached to withstand the « ordeal of reality » duty itself might be revealed as an over-sentimental concept, — but all natures do not possess irony. We will not attack the concept.

Whatever hardy beauty there be is inextricably united with law but it is distasteful that the law should be most in evidence. Therefore, Broadway, New-York, is a highly pleasing spectacle viewed at night. The more or less futile gesture of skyscrapers towards height is nuanced in darkness ; there is no infliction of law, engineering or moral, in the way electric signs rest high in the sky without even the shadow of a support visible. Contortionists

perform, kittens play, giants wrestle around a
circuit of lights. Globule on globule of coloured
brightness run their tracks over dim roofs, which
in turn, tower above the continual flow of crowds
coming, going, flowing, — to no destination that
one can judge.

And the imagination romances on from any
given point where actuality ceases ; — to sense the
dynamic whir and continual revolution of wheels
in the universe, wearing down time. —

Whether it is pleasing to reflect upon or not,
behind the lights, controlling the glamour, are
laws; but as has been suggested, one does not care
to be confronted by too austere and provincial an
interpretation of them, doubting as one does the
competence and insight of the interpreters. The
city lights go out, the smoke will pass, the little
evil one may do will evaporate at last.

MORALITY

There is much of the puritanical in the cold austerity of skyscrapers. Utilitarian morality only
entered into the problem of their erection. Yet in
their severity there contrives to be less gratifying
to the esthetic sense than in bare steel frames into
which the problem of comfort has not yet come.

Horizontal planes intersecting the vertical cut
designs against the ethereal sky's opacity, and set

against each other aided by oblique steel props, they form triangles, and conjunctive polyhedrals which seem fantastically to scheme a model chart for the entire infinity with the same logaritmic exactness as they themselves are planned.

Skyscrapers, in Amerîca, are always constructed towards that end which is popularly known as « practical », but I, an American — and I do not proclaim, or apologize, for that fact, being neither responsible for it, nor able to discover any one nation's quality immeasurably superior to any other — recall Coney Island, and intricate steel skeletons builded to permit the public novel amusement — which achieved novelty and the amusing because the public believed this so — and in recalling Coney Island after having seen Eiffel Tower, sense bleakly a value that is « eternal », much as I have sensed such a value in looking upon prehistoric remnants. There are other immortalities, one feels, than stupidity, sentimentality, and simplicity based on the routine of security in existence. The intricacy of inventively wrought gigantic steel skeletons makes hope less barren that complex existence too has a firm foundation. Gray, bleak, cold, decisive, they stand indominatably into the sky — soullessly, heartlessly, — perhaps — as are mountains and the sea — but their fascination clutches one as no redundant speach on spirituality can clutch.

For flesh is only a pulp that melts, mainly

moisture, but skeletons survive to be the history and the romance of the prehistoric for the post-historic. So it is with emotion! Which people readily acclaim, resenting, if not ignoring, the value of understanding which insists upon recognitions beyond mere sensual and sentimental desires.

PORTRAITS OF RELIGIOUS ONES

Futility walked in the train of any assurance to him that his prophetic furies, and the swirling of cosmic conceptions in his brain, were tricks of his psychologic organism — a trick common particularly to organisms engendered with Semetic blood. Caught in the currents of mystical, and to him altogether lovely promissory imaginations, he knew himself to be inspired. The murky and rich effluvia of his dreams' vapour exalted his brooding spirit, urging him on to be a force in the reconstruction of society. Why say the word « frustration » to him ? He had plenty to eat ; he had a wife.

It is thus that fanatics, ascetics, narrow but none the less dominating personalities, are wrought ; personalities whose fervor clings to preceding generations long after it is cold of passion, and serves in the aftertimes only to obstruct men's visions.

A conception of clear rationality which observes, relates, and understands, has also its strict limitations. There are always people who want experience to be ardorous with impulses and exaltations. Understanding is poor food for them.

The realization that the morality which guides the conduct of society is based on conventionalization of some Savonarolaic judgment causes one to despair of rationality in organization ; thus to believe that the force of such fresh frenetic fanaticism as this man's may effect desirable changes, or changes that are at least no more oppressive than the old order.

Though one chooses with one's mind to stand at some window looking out upon the spectacle, analyzing the designs, noting the colours, without the complex mental and spiritual confusion of participation, one is forced to acknowledge that life is not lived in the mind so that intelligent preferences fail to dominate many situations. At moments of such failure, men such as this one, spluttering, but striking out with passionate sincerity — if emotions are ever sincere — strike cords of sentiency and desire. Existence is so drab, so tedious, so utterly appalling in its stupidity that one can never quite accept it without smouldering protestation.

And it is not unlikely that the irritation at him, and at his cloying social sentimentality is also irritation of the intellect because of its own inability to ride through the heavy fog of his virulent argumentation into a region of clarity and solution.

FROSTED FRUIT

The man has been wounded often — but so have we all — though he declares himself to be invulnerable now. He was not meant to be a detached person however. It may not be invulnerability to have permitted one's continuing desires to have frozen to frustrations within one. One is well aware that this man is still quite personal in his reactions, so that he fails to set many experiences aside as « purely relative. » Their impact leaves wounds and impressions that are not always an addition to life uses. One must be sufficiently perceptive to see that his calm is an ice exterior over the lividity of many terrors.

There are irksome people who say lightly such terms as « coldly intellectual » and « lacking spontaneity ». Such people should visit an iron ore plant and discover what heat is needed to make steel. Emotions that blurt out in flames do not affect the sky for long, or devastate rock-hard prejudices.

This man would freeze flowing emotion into « something accomplished and done with. » He would have the frozen block for discreet usage in very hot weather. But things he has chosen to ignore are continually hindering him in his intentions.

18

FLAME OF « YOUTH »

Defiant, pliant boy, he so much wants to be essential, — a tragic egoist without the humour to understand that the world will never find one man as important to it as to himself; to know that stupidity is at least as secure as any other immortality. Young boys have cried out their anguish for centuries; they will not let themselves know that only such as suffer as they do will listen to their cries, and that but to join in the chorus. Life continues quite relentlessly, and it may be only a weak notion that relentlessness is not a merciful quality.

Cut like the brooding oval of some luminous sad-eyed Saint done in oils by an old Italian master, he sits with apathy, seared with inward protestations by his « spirituality », which is made of due portions of poverty, sex anguish, and environment which such natures as his can not dominate. He is bitter, and afraid, because men, and generations of men, and nations, are all of little importance, so that he himself cannot be highly valued. But he screams out yet. He has that happiness. One regrets the day when he will discover that screams attract no more attention where everything is noisy, than does calmness; when he will know that men do not treasure madness unless it be their own particular madness. It is difficult to conceive what faith will preserve him when his faith in madness, in screams, and in rage against the brutality of society, have departed. Defiant boy, some blindness will always be in him to protect him.

A POETESS

She is a starved woman — which does not distinguish her — but her starvation is for food, mere food. Too she craves « recognition ». — But her starvation is best described not qualified.

A malnutrite saint politician, bitter through never having realized purification, she writes songs from the urge within her. Her songs do not satisfy her. She is hungry. She does not want sympathy, and the cold purity of understanding chills her to the marrow.

No one can help her. She must express herself and after all these years life can no longer be simple. She must insist upon her « spiritual hungers », saying « you have not read my poem to the end. It was not sweet but quite vicious there. How little you understand not to think me sincere. » Then she reaches out spiritual talons and goes on groping and grasping, starvedly. She can not know that starvation has always made sincerity a concept only.

It is the over–sensitive ones alone who are ill at ease when she recites. They say that she creates an atmosphere of tragic denunciation that insists too greatly upon itself.

Somedays the conscious intensity drops from her and she is only hungry, and weary of being hungry. Then she is distant, aloof towards life for playing the snob with her.

SALESMANSHIP

For an entire day in the Pullman he had been reading « Sales Methods ». Sometimes a flush of eagerness on his cheeks unified the red splotches of his complexion. Then his weak eyes glistened so that his black slouch hat was not needed to shade their uncertainty. His protruding lips would fall open with a zest to gulp faster the knowledge he sipped into his brain. He was so despicably, weakly, hopeful.

It is well for his peace of mind that he did not know a college professor, forced to teaching by consecutive failures in business had written this book which was to make him a power in the business world. But when he would discover that there would always be some correspondence course to lure him on, yearning for competency.

STRONG MEN

Whether it is lumber or coal which they unload from the barges they do it with great ease. Three of them came to work drunk Monday morning; several of the rest were not drunk simply because liquor didn't take them that way. All but two of them were good tempered, ready to be joshed and kidded, and to return the obscene joviality with alacrity. Their intoxication did not interfere with the amount of work they got through; or did the overalls of one of the men who apparently had no waistline, and whose undersuit seemed to weigh his pants of as they sagged.

One wouldn't praise the beauty of their physiques, because the dust and perspiration, as well as the dirtiness of their loose garments hid any beauty anyone of them might have. Some had knotty muscles; others were smooth of brawn. They unload lumber, or coal, all week. On Saturdays such of them as drink their wages go out and secure rot-gut whiskey. It is the same with the lumberjacks from Minnesota who work all winter in camp and who in the spring go to Minneapolis and spend all their wages in a drunkon, till some night they pawn the new clothes they have bought and have to return to camp and a long winter job again, and no women to sleep with.

If there is anything remarkable about them it must be their muscles; no, no, it must be the casual way they take life and don't give a goddam. Not faithful, not plodding animals, still they get much work done, and think nothing of it. And they are not stupid people. Some of them think rapidly and observe minutely. I never know what to think of human beings.

THE PENNY

Peter took the quarter which his mother handed him and started to the grocery store. Through a sensitive impulse of embarrassment, and also because of fear of refusal, he did not ask his mother for a penny to spend.

Guilt already lay the weight of its great body upon him, for in his under consciousness was a formed intention, — hopeful and fearful.

Times come in the experience of the will when to act or to fail act at its bidding are equal breakdowns. The will having strained, has with the torment of straining set up resistences to impulse that are themselves impulses, so much burdened with willing that the ability to make decisions is lost. The taunt of daring to do and the sense of duty not to do balance each other.

Peter had arrived at such a point in his willing life. For six years he had accepted without question the routine of life inflicted upon him by his parents, because he had not known that it was possible to resist this routine. Only the last year, with schoolmates, had other possibilities been revealed to him.

One day he had nearly lied to his mother about a tardiness in reaching home. At the last moment his heart expanded almost to the point of explosion however, so that in his self-consciousness and presense of guilt he blurted out the truth and stolidly took a spanking.

Right now he craved candy. Fear of refusal had kept him from asking his mother for a penny from change which he would recive after buying her a can of tomatoes. More than the fear however, he was held from asking her by the knowledge that he could pay but 18 c. for the tomatoes instead of 20 c. and thus have two pennies to spend.

At the store when he told the clerk to give him « that can of tomatoes » he was sure the clerk looked at him accusingly. He wondered if evil impulses ever came to the clerk, who looked so at peace with the world, and with his conscience. They surely could not. God's heart must be twitching with pain for him, Peter thought, and with disgust and anger too.

The candy which he purchased tasted like glue in his mouth at one moment, when mingling with the unsavory flavour of his conscience. He devoured it all however, and returned home.

That night he prayed fervently to God to forgive him. For a long time he was awake thinking that surely on the to morrow his mother would have discovered his guilt, and her discovery he feared. God at least could be placated by prayer.

Several days passed, and Peter prayed every night to be forgiven. He began to doubt that his mother would ever find out about his offense. Neither did God do anything whatever about it, and Peter had expected an unmistakable reproof.

He would look up in the sky, and wonder if the day would ever be clear enough so that he could see God sitting on his throne, with Jesus standing near him, and angels flying all over heaven. God's throne must be an easy rocking chair, from which he gave forth commands, having Jesus or some angel bring him his easy slippers, fill his pipe, and attend to his needs always. Perhaps God had been asleep when he took the pennies, Jimmy concluded.

Three months went by. Peter had discovered that Santa Claus was only his father dressed up. When he asked his mother about this she smiled and said: « Santa Claus is in your own heart, Peter, if you have the right kind of heart. »

She had said the same thing was true about God too, almost the same thing.

How either Santa Claus or God could be in his heart without his feeling them, Peter failed to understand. He was sure now that he did not love either one of them. They were too much like his father, too much the symbols of denied impulses for that. He was rather afraid of his father.

At last Peter stopped praying his little extra prayer, after going to bed, to be forgiven for steal-ing the pennies. He only said his regular prayers because his mother would have scolded him other-wise. Somehow, he knew not why or how, she had deceived him about God, for her own ends, he felt.

When on clear days he looked up in the sky and recalled that one older boy had said you could travel a thousand lifetimes and never get through the sky, he would decide it wasn't possible to think how deep the sky really is. It wouldn't be possible for God, the father, to sit all over that amount of space, or to know what everyone everywhere is is doing.

So Peter began to take other pennies from his mother, and forget to pray about taking them. Any desire to be good had departed from him. He was simply careful not to be so bad that people would remark on his being a bad, bad boy.

TRUANT

Clear sky bright all the way down from unspeakably high up with a nymphlike wind running down it across the garden of red and yellow tulips, running irresponsibly with tulips to the lakeshore past the meadow. When he runs it runs with him and they are dancing, both lightly but never caught up with each other and never out of breath together, but the air is happy, and the air is clear, so he is happy too — but

« Have to mow that damned old lawn. »

« Have to weed that damned old garden... No. Will not. Get a licking from dad sure, but get a licking anyway. »

There. The young white dove that has a sore wing, and whose beak is pale because it's sick perhaps. Sweetheart dove. Kiss its poor head. Poor little dove. « Just you sit on my shoulder and cuddle your head in my neck and go to sleep with your eyes. I won't let the chickens peck at you any more, never ».

The day is shiny bright coloured glass that is flowing with flowers, bubbling into clear cool images of happy moments that break, but more bubbles come. Forget the garden; forget the lawn; forget father, forget mother. Tell stories to self; about doves and a garden of flowers, and a woods with foliage weeping down in strings of coloured lace leaves, and branches full of birds and only the kind of people that are lovely and merry.

Creation

A Protoplasmic Farce

Stage Setting : Nothing : really a very simple conception. You should readily have it in your mind.

As an aid : Recall some night when you slept heavily, a black, dreamless sleep, for eight hours. All night long you were thinking : Nothing : Remember that then : Nothing:

ACT I

Nothing slowly condenses. Finally — no time elapses, there is not yet time ; there is nothing! — A tiny mass of protoplasm without any colour whatever appears. There is no motion within the interiors of the protoplasm. Only the possibilities of growth.

ACT II

What is this protoplasm for ? To have life. So ? It must have consciousness then, but of what. Self? Then it must have a consciousness of something other than self. It must — feel.

(Someone is surely directing this drama. Already we have lost the conception of nothing. O well, we shall get other conceptions of as little consequence as we proceed into life.)

ACT III

The great vastness of nothingness has been tapped, and through the siphoning tube ethery clouds of condensed nothing are pouring. Condensed variously, many things are obtained — pain sorrow, joy, etc. By putting a little of each of these into the mass of protoplasm we will secure a full consciousness surely. After they have diffused into the protoplasm thoroughly it shall divide, and propagate continually.

None of you spectators of this drama know what feeling — joy, or sorrow is. Your understanding is limited to the small portion of feeling which you have yourselves experienced.

From nothingness had come everything. Peace is eternally barred from being. Vague Shadows, or premonitions of what might ultimately be shadows fall upon the quivering masses of protoplasm. The dominant premonition is experience. Gad! the dour viciousness, the buccaneering slap-stick comedianism of that villain, experience.

Even before coming upon the stage it has conspired with religion, morality, tradition — and the triple arch-villain, purity. So time and space come upon the stage like ministering angels to alleviate the unbearable tedium which these villains will inflict upon the infantile protoplasm. So the nuclear forms become aged with youth, since the time when time began.

ACT IV

Light and color fall upon the nucleoplasmic colony which quivers and trembles in time and space. Sex, which was one of the passions filtered from nothingness, lures various members of the colony to each other. To preserve experience, and to grant the plasms ability to learn habit-reactions, neuronic systems are evolved, from the cask of nothingness. Instincts that emerge into intuitions and finally into intelligence appear.

With light comes darkness. To every positive a negative. Purity and intelligence are followed in natural sequence by filth and stupidity. The intelligent sees everything as ineffably pure, mysterious, beautiful — that is, good: the stupid questions everything as something to evade, suspect as vile and hideous, best defeated by pretending unconsciousness of its presence.

> Sun, Cold–Heavens, Stars
> And Rainbows;
> Gold leaf studded
> With bleeding carbuncle,
> And rose diamond on
> Platinum in jade velvet.
> Golden pheasant tails
> Were meant to drag in mire,
> Else what proves them rare!
> The circles in a peacock's tail
> Are absolute worlds,
>   silver fires circling
>   syncopated intentions
>   revolving.

Tear a nerve
from the spine
of creation.
Draw it taut
like the catgut
of a sad violin.
It will shriek
in tormented
anguish.
   That is music.
   Living things,
   Nerve fraught all,
   sympathize
   and enjoy.

So naked protoplasms
clothe themselves
in conscious
      form
      colour
      sound
which exudes forth
and the peace
      and silence
      are broken
         forever.

So the curtain is drawn discreetly, so as to no
further fetter anticipation by experience.

You may write dramas of your own, conceive
Gods and growing plants as you will, and seek to
grasp infinity into your mind, if the genius is with
you, an impersonal interest drives you to the effort,
you have a naïve faith in the ultimate intelligence
of men, — thus are encouraged to articulate.

TABLE OF CONTENTS

· DIJON — DARANTIERE

RETURN
TO ➡

CIRCULATION DEPARTMENT
202 Main Library

LOAN PERIOD 1

RETURN
TO ➡

CIRCULATION DEPARTMENT
202 Main Library

LOAN PERIOD 1

4

5

6

2

3

642-3403

LIBRARY USE

DUE AS STAMPED BELOW

This book is due before closing time on the last date stamped below

REC. CIR. NOV 2 '78

OCT 1 9 2002

FEB 14 2002

UNIVERSITY OF CALIFORNIA LIBRARY

FORM NO. DD 6, 40m 10'77

UNIVERSITY OF CALIFORNI
BERKELEY, CA 947

ImTheStory.com

Personalized Classic Books in many genre's

Unique gift for kids, partners, friends, colleagues

Customize:

- Character Names

- Upload your own front/back cover images (optional)

- Inscribe a personal message/dedication on the

  inside page (optional)

Customize many titles Including
- Alice in Wonderland
- Romeo and Juliet
- The Wizard of Oz
- A Christmas Carol
- Dracula
- Dr. Jekyll & Mr. Hyde
- And more...

Lightning Source UK Ltd.
Milton Keynes UK
UKHW02f1944051217
313944UK00016B/792/P

9 781314 829082